AF718975

PRODUCTIVITY AND QUALITY: MEASUREMENT AS A BASIS FOR IMPROVEMENT

EVERETT E. ADAM, JR.
University of Missouri-Columbia

JAMES C. HERSHAUER
Arizona State University

WILLIAM A. RUCH
Arizona State University

PRENTICE-HALL, INC., Englewood Cliffs, New Jersey 07632

Library of Congress Cataloging in Publication Data

Adam, Everett E.
Productivity and quality.

Bibliography: p.
Includes index.
1. Industrial productivity–Measurement.
2. Quality of products–Measurement. 3. Banks and banking–Labor productivity. I. Hershauer, James C. II. Ruch, William A. III. Title.
HD56.A3 658.3'14 81-5118
ISBN 0-13-725002-9 AACR2

Editorial/production supervision and interior design by Lori E. Wieseneck and Steven Young
Cover design by Edsal Enterprises
Manufacturing buyer: Gordon Osbourne and Ed O'Dougherty

HD
56
.A3

©1981 by Prentice-Hall, Inc., Englewood Cliffs, N.J. 07632

All rights reserved. No part of this book may be reproduced in any form or by any means without permission in writing from the publisher.

Printed in the United States of America

10 9 8 7 6 5 4 3 2 1

Prentice-Hall International, Inc., *London*
Prentice-Hall of Australia Pty. Limited, *Sydney*
Prentice-Hall of Canada, Ltd., *Toronto*
Prentice-Hall of India Private Limited, *New Delhi*
Prentice-Hall of Japan, Inc., *Tokyo*
Prentice-Hall of Southeast Asia Pte. Ltd., *Singapore*
Whitehall Books Limited, Wellington, *New Zealand*

Contents

Preface

Although productivity is widely discussed today, the concept is not so widely understood. This is due in part to the complexity of issues surrounding and affecting productivity. We intend through this book first to promote an understanding of productivity as it relates to quality and, second, to provide ways to develop productivity-quality measurements for service functions within all types of organizations.

Productivity improvement is an extremely complex and vitally important subject. Productivity must include a quality dimension, for if a firm increases quantity at the cost of lower quality, it gains little, if any, overall productivity. To improve the quantity and quality dimensions of productivity, each organization will likely have to merge a great many tools, techniques, and methods forming a unique improvement program of its own. Evaluating the productivity improvement program and ensuring its eventual success depend upon the ability to measure both productivity and quality in service as well as manufacturing functions. Thus, measurement is a basis, a prerequisite, for improvement.

It is beyond the scope of this book to explore the many productivity improvement techniques. We intend to promote productivity-quality improvement by providing guidelines for the development of measurement systems.

For the manager interested in an overview of quality measures for productivity, we recommend concentrating primarily on Chapters 1, 2, and 7. For the specialist responsible for creating productivity measures, we detail a process that develops measurement systems in Chapter 3. Chapter 4 clarifies the process by explaining productivity results in a quasi-manufacturing function (check processing) and an internal service function (personnel) in Federal Reserve banks. Chapters 5 and 6 provide conceptual models and related hypotheses for productivity researchers, but the material in these chapters can also help the improvement specialist determine what factors should be controlled by specific programs. Academics interested in hypothesis generation and testing might be most interested in parts of Chapters 2 and 3, the conceptual models of Chapters 5 and 6, and applications in Chapter 7.

We are deeply indebted to the National Science Foundation and staff for the support of our research efforts and the permission to include results in this book. We would like to give special recognition to Dr. Richard O. Mason, formerly Program Manager of the National Science Foundation and currently a faculty member at the University of Southern California.

The special contributions of David C. Lincoln, who funded our original work in productivity and who continually encourages and supports productivity improvement, we gratefully acknowledge. Administrative and support staff at our universities--the University of Missouri-Columbia and Arizona State University--have always provided valuable support and assistance in our research efforts that led to this book. We particularly thank Dr. Thomas Fullmer, Director of ASU's Productivity Institute.

Professor Richard B. Chase of the University of Arizona and Professor James Taylor of the University of California at Los Angeles gave valuable consulting advice as we were designing the measurement process. Three Federal Reserve banks participated in the research results given in Chapter 4. Executives, managers, supervisors, and workers unselfishly donated their time and expertise. Additionally, an outstanding review panel and numerous other academic, business, and governmental leaders provided advice and assistance. Since some of these individuals must remain anonymous, we would like to thank them as a group for their major contributions to this book.

Most importantly, we would like to acknowledge the creative efforts of managers and employees working in business and government who have shown a strong interest in improving our productivity efforts. Successful applications of this measurement procedure have been accomplished by such leadership. Several individuals and organizations, primarily in banking and high technology firms, are recognized in Chapter 7, which discusses their applications.

Everett E. Adam, Jr.
James C. Hershauer
William A. Ruch

1
Introduction

Productivity is the life blood of our economy and the foundation for our standard of living. The United States claims only 7 percent of the world's land and 6 percent of the world's population, yet it produces one third of the world's goods and services. During this century, productivity increases have been responsible for reducing the workweek by one half and by adding six years of leisure time to the average American's life. The world leadership that the United States once held, however, is rapidly eroding; productivity in other industrialized nations has been far exceeding our annual increases in per capita output. We fully appreciate the importance of productivity, but we are just beginning to realize the difficulty of maintaining sustained growth.

Worker productivity is often discussed, often misunderstood, much maligned, and vitally important. The following statements are derived from many of the commonly held opinions regarding worker productivity:

> Worker productivity is the key to economic viability and increased wealth.
>
> Worker productivity is improved by capital investment.

Worker productivity is improved by labor specialization and job design.

Worker productivity is improved when labor works harder.

Worker productivity is improved when labor works smarter, not harder.

Worker productivity increases mean work speed-up and exploitation of labor.

Worker productivity increases are a primary determinant of job elimination and unemployment.

Worker productivity increases are opposed by labor unions.

Worker productivity refers to the output of direct labor in manufacturing jobs.

Worker productivity is a function of the workers' performing the task.

Worker productivity is a function of management practices and policies.

Worker productivity is a function of pay.

Worker productivity is a function of the environment.

Worker productivity is a function of a complex system of interrelated variables: individual, organizational, and environmental.

These statements provoke debate concerning their truth and applicability depending upon the background and orientation of the individuals involved and their definition of terms. The only general conclusion that can be drawn from the many articles, speeches, government resolutions, conferences, case studies, and research efforts is that we are just now beginning to realize how important, yet how complex, is the subject of "worker productivity."

The subject of "productivity" often evokes emotional, polarized reactions from labor, management, stockholders, and consumers. News stories and advertisements point out the importance of productivity and the great need for increasing the level of output to maintain, if not increase, the standard of living and the quality of working life. Yet it is apparent that much more is said about productivity than is known on the basis of sound research and theory.

ANTECEDENTS OF THE PRODUCTIVITY PROBLEM

To gain some perspective on the present milieu requires a brief examination of some of the major historical developments leading to the creation of the current preoccupation with productivity. Certainly, the Industrial Revolution and the movement away from an agrarian society was the pivotal point in history that instigated the concern with worker output. The major factors that have impinged on productivity since the mid-nineteenth century include the development of a demanding work ethic, the scientific management movement, the growth of labor unions, the human relations school of thought, and the accelerating advancements in technology. Furthermore, the role of government has been changing; it has begun to control the interaction among labor, management, stockholders, and consumers by using Keynesian theories to attempt to govern the economy. Today, neo-Keynesian theories are being challenged as inadequate. Inflation, unemployment, and recession are occurring simultaneously, a condition not predicted by any contemporary theory. Developments in economic theory and the future role of government vis-a-vis the economy are uncertain at present.

<u>The Changing Work Ethic</u>. The nineteenth century was a period of development for the "work ethic" as <u>the</u> primary reason for the very existence of man. At this time in history, it is difficult to separate the work ethic from the Protestant ethic, which, together, made work and not leisure the acceptable activity of God-fearing people. A job required the total commitment of a person's working hours to fulfill often overwhelming job duties. Job descriptions characteristic of this period even indicated the time for morning prayers and the time allotted for courting. Observing the societal changes that have occurred since that time, it is not surprising that we are dealing with a changing work ethic; most remarkable is the fact that the old work ethic lasted into the mid-twentieth century with some relevance!

<u>The Scientific Management Movement</u>. Frederick W. Taylor's philosophy of work design so pervaded industrial manufacturing that he is credited with initiating a major school of thought in the theory and practice of

production. Although specialization and division of labor are truly ancient concepts, Taylor greatly refined these ideas in a world that had the motive to increase productive output and was developing the technology to implement it. Taylor found the "one best way" to perform a task by eliminating unnecessary operations or movements, by specializing and subdividing tasks, and by blending the optimum use of labor with the optimum amount of capital equipment.

In Principles of Scientific Management, Taylor (1917) said, "the greatest prosperity can exist only as the result of the greatest possible productivity of the men and machines of the establishment." Speaking to a group of managers and scholars, he stated his case even more strongly:

> The immense increase in the productivity of man marks the difference between civilized and uncivilized countries, marks the one great advance we have made on 100 to 200 years ago; it is due to that increase in productivity that the working people of today, with all the talk about their misery and their horrible treatment, live almost as well as kings did 250 years ago. They have better food, better clothing, and on the whole more comforts than kings had 250 years ago. And that is due to just one thing, increase of output. (1911)

Apparently Taylor's words were believed, for the result of his efforts was to build a professional society, indeed a movement, of followers that was international in scope and fervent in belief about the need for increasing productivity. Although some say that his ideas have been carried to an extreme of overspecialization, there is no doubt that Taylor's philosophy still shapes the design of many jobs today.

The Human Relations Movement. Whereas Taylor was primarily concerned with the method by which workers performed their tasks, the human relations proponents focused on the psychosociology of the workers themselves. Having begun by experimenting with the working conditions, it soon became evident that the more powerful influences of productivity lay in subtle variables within the workers themselves, rather than in the environment. As with the Taylorian school, some of the concepts and theories were newly discovered, but much of their work involved the application of existing knowledge of human behavior to an industrial setting. Although some conflict between these two schools of thought was inevitable, in concert they provided a more complete approach to productivity increases. Job design theories led to increases in the potential output of a task, and human relations concepts were employed to realize that potential over time.

The Growth of Labor Unions. During the time that these two schools of thought were being developed, organized labor was making considerable progress toward equalizing the balance of power between mnagement and labor. Nowhere was this more evident than in the growth and development of industrial unions. It is not coincidental that industries able to implement major productivity increases were also those industries that became the target of organized labor. As the pie to be divided became bigger, the sharing of that pie became a more critical issue. Management's prerogative with respect to the implementation of changes designed to improve productivity was lessened by the strength of organized labor.

Unions were not and are not opposed to productivity increases. They do attempt, however, to represent the total interests of the worker, and they say that they are opposed to "work speed-ups that are disguised as productivity gains." In addition, unions represent the workers in their claim to reap their share of the benefits of any gain in productivity. Finally, unions are concerned that the striving for higher productivity is not accomplished at the cost of the quality of working life. Productivity gains are important, but not so important that some workers must endure extreme physical or psychological hardships for the third of their lives spent on the job.

The power that organized labor wields in the bargaining process can, therefore, take any of several forms. It can be manifest in resistance to changes that would make the job more productive but are deemed not in the total interest of the worker. It can be simply a claim for more pay and benefits to share in the productivity increase or to offset the undesirable aspects of the changes. Ultimately, if other efforts fail, unions can derive their share by reducing the amount of time spent on the job through shorter working hours, more and longer vacations, and earlier retirement. By their presence, organized labor groups compel management to integrate the best of both the Taylorian principles of work design with the more subtly beneficial but less measurable principles of the human behavioralists.

Advancements in Technology. Technological innovation is an unending process. Technological advancement in this decade is proceeding at a more rapid rate than it did in the previous decade, but that statement can be made about every past time period and probably about every future period. Technological changes can improve productivity; a farmer can produce more with a tractor than with a team of horses. However, advancing technology does not necessarily increase productivity. The introduction of new capital equipment may significantly change the nature of the job to be done and may interact in unforeseen ways with the other factors of production. The farmer who trades his or her horses for a tractor must also master new mechanical skills and develop new techniques of planting and cultivation.

The cost of increased productivity is sometimes technological unemployment. This phenomenon may be obvious in a developing nation that tries to enter the twentieth century too quickly, but its manifestations in American industry are much more subtle. We may recognize isolated cases of technological unemployment but be unaware of the many instances of technological inefficiency. As technological improvements change the nature of the job, the worker's competence may be gradually eroded to the point where additional capital equipment will not yield the expected benefits to productivity. A material handler in a stockroom is highly competent in moving materials by hand because of physical ability, strength, and a mental set that equates work with sweat. The addition of mechanical moving equipment brings the handler closer to being a truck driver but still uses some of the handler's physical abilities. A further refinement to an automated, computerized material retrieval system makes physical skills unimportant and cognitive skills paramount. The stock handler may not be unemployed because of the changes, but that same handler may be technologically inefficient by failing to develop both the skills and the attitude necessary to perform a completely different job than the one for which he or she was hired.

The point is not to argue for or against technological improvements or to bemoan the fact that technological unemployment is sometimes inevitable. The point is to emphasize the systems approach to productivity improvement by first recognizing that no one factor--job redesign, human relations techniques, or technological changes--can be successfully implemented without due consideration given to the many factors that influence productivity and their complex and often subtle interactions.

The Changing Role of Government. Government has had an important, albeit often indirect, influence on productivity. Labor legislation, consumer protection regulations, and even tax regulations may redirect the way in which factors of production are allocated. If unions are given more protection or more power under the law, they may effectively block changes they feel are not in the best interest of the workers they represent. If consumers are protected by more accurate labeling, by safety devices, or by obtaining more effective legal recourse for defective products, then productivity is influenced either in terms of cost or in units.

Stockholders influence productivity through the voting right given to the ownership of a corporation. Management influences productivity by virtue of the authority given it by the owners. Labor exerts its influence through organization and collective bargaining. Consumers influence productivity by "casting votes" in the marketplace. Each group has the ability to influence productivity, although some obviously have a more powerful and more direct impact. It is the role of government to maintain that balance of power so that productivity increases can be made in such a way that each group shares equitably in both the benefits and the costs of higher productivity.

Past studies of productivity have tended to focus on one or a few of the many factors that influence the output of goods and services. Only through such concentration can a particular aspect be examined with sufficient depth to yield understanding. This concentration on a single factor, however, can also lead to an academic myopia with respect to the way in which these many factors interact to yield productivity gains or losses.

NATIONAL PRODUCTIVITY

Productivity is a ratio of outputs to inputs. At the national level, output represents all goods and services produced in the private sector measured in constant dollars. Input is limited to labor only; it is the sum of all hours worked in the private sector weighted by different wage rates and salary levels. This ratio is a partial productivity measure that indicates the effectiveness and efficiency of the use of labor in the production of salable goods and services. It is, of course, influenced by advancements in technology, changes in the labor-capital ratio, effective or ineffective management practices, worker motivation, and many other factors.

The United States is the most productive nation in the Free World by this measure; however, the growth rate of U.S. productivity is the slowest. In the post-World War II period up to the late 1960s, productivity increased an average of 3.2 percent per year. In the early 1970s, the average annual rate dropped to 1.4 percent, influenced partly by a major recession in 1973-1974. Productivity growth failed to return to its previous level, however; in 1978 growth was only 0.5 percent and in 1979 productivity fell by almost a full 1.0 percent. Without a major change in productivity growth rates, the U.S. will soon lose its leadership and find the productivity of five or more countries greater than U.S. productivity by the end of the 1980s.

Various reasons have been offered for this decline, including increased government regulations, reduced levels of R&D and investment, changes in the characteristics of the work force, environmental expenditures, and the shift from a manufacturing to a service economy. Although each of these is important and should be addressed, the ultimate source of productivity improvement is within the firm itself, through the effective and efficient management of resources. The American Productivity Center of Houston, Texas, a privately funded, nonprofit organization, is making considerable progress in developing and disseminating information on increasing firm productivity.

Increasingly, top management is becoming concerned with productivity. Increasing costs, lower profit margins, and pressure from foreign competition have made management aware of the need for better resource utilization. Specifically, they want to know:

1. What is productivity; how is it defined?
2. How is productivity measured and how does it differ from traditional profit, return on investment, or other financial measures?
3. How is it improved?

The focus of this book is on the first two of these questions as necessary prerequisites to beginning to answer question 3. In this chapter, definitions of productivity and quality are developed, and the relationships between the two are explained. The critical relationship between productivity and profit is also discussed.

The remainder of the book emphasizes quality measurement within a productivity framework (i.e., output relative to input). Hypothetical examples are used to explain the measurement development procedure, but data from several applications of the procedure in real organizations are also presented.

The third question, how to improve productivity--particularly the quality dimension--is beyond the scope of this book. Many theories, ideas, and techniques have been tried with varying degrees of success but it is clear that, without measurement, improvement efforts cannot be properly evaluated. Measurement, therefore, forms a basis for improvement through evaluation of applications of many different techniques. The measurement system described here should permit more progress toward the establishment of practical and effective productivity improvement efforts.

A DEFINITION OF PRODUCTIVITY

National productivity has been defined as total output relative to labor input. For some purposes, this definition is adequate, but, at the firm level, labor must be balanced with other productive resources in a combination that is both feasible and profitable. A general definition of firm productivity is suggested:

> Productivity is a systemic concept concerning the conversion of inputs to outputs by the system under consideration.

This dynamic concept can be defined more specifically as outputs relative to the four major resource inputs of the firm:

$$\text{Productivity} = \frac{\text{Outputs}}{\text{Labor} + \text{capital} + \text{materials} + \text{energy}} \qquad (1\text{-}1)$$

Productivity so defined may be referred to as total productivity. Outputs relative to only one, two, or three of the inputs are partial measures of productivity. Output per labor hour, tons shipped per employee, customers served per payroll dollar, units produced per kilowatt hour, and other similar ratios are all partial productivity measures.[1]

---

[1] Many articles and books have been prepared on company productivity measurement. For a more complete discussion, the interested reader might see Douglas L. Cocks, "The Measurement of Total Factor Productivity for a Large U.S. Manufacturing Corporation," *Business Economics*, September, 1974; John W. Kendrick and Daniel Creamer, *Measuring Company Productivity*, rev. ed., The Conference Board Studies in Business Economics, No. 89, 1975; and Irving H. Siegel, *Company Productivity: Measurement for Improvement* (Kalamazoo, Mich.: Upjohn Institute, 1980).

PRODUCTIVITY AND PROFITABILITY

Productivity and profitability are not the same thing, although there is a close relationship between the two. Normally, if productivity increases, profits will also increase. It is possible, however, for one to be increasing while the other is decreasing.

Increasing productivity and falling profits may reflect a technologically advancing industry in a very tight market. Many electronics firms, for example, are producing many more calculators with fewer resources, yet are finding that their profit margins are dwindling. The firm must be content with the understanding that without the productivity gains it would not have a chance of competing in that market.

The opposite situation--declining productivity and increasing profits--is very dangerous to the economy. It means that resources are being less well utilized and that the inefficiencies are being passed on to the customer. The firm is lulled into a feeling of being successful, yet it is contributing to inflation and becoming more vulnerable to competition, either foreign or domestic.

The relationship between profit and productivity can be explained with a profitability ratio of sales to costs. Sales are made up of a variety of output quantities each times its respective price. Similarly, costs are the total of each input quantity (labor, capital, material, and energy) times its respective unit cost (wage rate, cost per square foot, etc.). Thus,

$$\frac{\text{Sales}}{\text{Costs}} = \frac{\text{Output quantities x prices}}{\text{Input quantities x unit costs}} \tag{1-2}$$

which is equivalent to:

$$\frac{\text{Sales}}{\text{Costs}} = \frac{\text{Output quantities}}{\text{Input quanitities}} \times \frac{\text{Prices}}{\text{Unit costs}} \tag{1-3}$$

The first of the two ratios on the right-hand side is productivity. If costs and prices are held constant, it tells how well inputs are being used to produce outputs. The second ratio is called price recovery. It tells the degree to which output prices are keeping up with changes in input unit costs.

If a firm compares its performance year by year, changes in profit must be accounted for by a change in productivity, a change in price recovery, or a combination of the two. If price recovery remains constant, changes in profit are a direct function of changes in productivity, and the reverse is also true. It can also be seen in this framework, however, that a slight change in either ratio can be more than offset by a relatively larger change in the other.[2]

The firm that maintains its profit through productivity increases will likely survive in the long run. The firm that depends only on an increasing price recovery ratio will survive only for as long as its competition permits.

PRODUCTIVITY AND QUALITY

Frequently, scholars and practitioners alike refer to "productivity" and "quality" as if they were two separate performance measures. Yet a significant part of any productivity equation is quality. There is no economic value in increased output levels if the increase is offset by lower quality.

Any study of productivity should measure output as the number of usable, salable, acceptable goods or services produced. Unfortunately, this is not always done. In fact, many operations are carefully monitored for "productivity" with no provision for detecting, measuring, or reporting errors or defects in output. In those studies where quantity and quality are considered, evidence illustrates that quantity-quality trade-offs are not straightforward but, rather, are moderated by intervening variables.

---

[2]See Irving H. Siegel, Company Productivity: Measurement for Improvement (Kalamazoo, Mich.: Upjohn Institute, 1980), Appendix note 1, pp. 77-79, for an alternative discussion of quantity and price forms of a productivity index.

The term "quality" suffers from some of the same problems as does the term "productivity." In the vernacular, a "quality" product often means the best--usually the most expensive model in a group of similar products or services. Thus, a Rolls Royce is a "quality" automobile, and the Four Seasons is a "quality" restaurant. To those responsible for the quality of an organization's product or service, however, a much more precise definition is needed. It may refer to the tolerances set up on the output or the percentage of units that meets those tolerances. A vast number of different precise definitions of quality are available to reflect different product or service characteristics, different measurement techniques, and different ways of expressing standards.

A general definition of quality must fall between the general understanding of the term and the very specific technical usage of the term if it is to be operational. It must be sufficiently precise to permit measurement and reporting of data in specific applications, yet sufficiently general to be applied to a wide variety of product and service attributes. Within these objectives, the following definition of quality is offered:

> Quality is the degree to which a product or service conforms to a set of predetermined standards related to the characteristics that determine its value in the marketplace and its performance of the function for which it was designed.

A definition of quality must meet several key tests. These tests are referred to as basic classifications of quality; they are really tests of definition generality.

The first classification is dichotomous rather than continuous (in statistical sampling, it is "attributes" versus "variables"). Dichotomous characteristics are seen as binary. The characteristics are either good or bad, acceptable or unacceptable, present or absent. Continuous characteristics, on the other hand, constitute factors that fall at some point on a scale. The scale may or may not be measurable. The key difference is that the attribute is not naturally dichotomous. For example, a light bulb may function or not function.

That characteristic is dichotomous. The intensity of the light from bulbs that do function, however, is a continuous characteristic, measurable in lumens. Arbitrary limits on the intensity scale must be set to establish an acceptable range.

This definition of quality covers both of these situations. "The degree to which a product or service conforms . . ." may be answered with yes or no, or it may be answered with a variance.

A second major quality classification is the reference to a specific unit as opposed to a lot or group of units. This definition can refer to a single unit of a product or service by indicating how that unit meets or fails to meet established criteria. It applies equally well, however, to the average variance from standard of a group of items or the percentage defective in a lot. The quality of the light bulbs, for example, could be expressed as the number that function out of every thousand manufactured.

Another classification of quality characteristics is in terms of functional and aesthetic attributes. A functional attribute directly affects the performance of the product or service. An aesthetic attribute affects the appearance or some other characteristic that, if defective, makes the product or service less desirable in the marketplace but does not hamper performance of the intended function. A bad valve will affect the function of an automobile; a bad paint job will not. This definition of quality takes both factors into account.

A fourth division of quality characteristics is measurable versus judgmental. Such attributes as size, temperature, voltage, or torque are easily measurable. Standards are therefore set in terms of these measurements and are accurately communicated to the technicians responsible for making the measurements. Taste, appearance, and other subjective characteristics may only be judged by the expert who decides if the unit meets the standard. Some characteristics, such as color, are measurable, but a judgmental process may be used to avoid the high cost of precise measurements. In this definition of quality, "standard" and "degree of conformance" may refer to either measurable or judgmental processes.

A final quality characteristic to be considered is the often overlooked attribute of timeliness. Frequently, this attribute is associated with services rather than with products, but it should be applied to both. Work at a construction site, for example, can be stopped by defective material; but it can also be stopped if the material is late in arriving. A product or service that is not in the right place at the right time can be classified as "defective" just as one that is timely but unacceptable. Because time is a continuous scale, timeliness can be expressed within this definition of quality as an additional standard with a range of acceptability.

FORMAT FOR THE BOOK

This introductory chapter has highlighted the nature of the problem and has offered definitions of the concepts of productivity and quality. The remainder of the book focuses on measurement of these concepts as a basis for improvement. It draws upon conceptualization and research from a variety of methodologies.

It is beyond the scope of this book to cover the techniques for improvement of quality. Often, quality management involves technical factors unique to the industry or firm being considered. Almost always, however, quality is also affected by the behavior of employees in the organization, by organizational policy, and by basic technological factors such as the type and age of equipment and the quality of raw materials. The conceptual models presented later are intended to provide a general understanding of the nature of the problem and to guide the use of specific techniques to improve quality in a given situation.

A necessary prerequisite for the improvement of productivity and quality is measurement. Attempting to employ specific quality improvement techniques without measurement and feedback of results is futile; it is not sound management practice.

The purpose of this book, therefore, is to provide direction in the measurement of productivity and quality to enable the effective evaluation of improvement techniques.

Part I centers on measuring the quality dimension of productivity. Within this part, Chapter 2 contains explanations of measures of both productivity and quality. Chapter 3 outlines a procedure for developing situation-specific measures within an organization. That procedure was developed under a grant from the National Science Foundation and was tested in the check-processing and personnel departments of three Federal Reserve banks. The results of that testing and the specific measures developed are explained in Chapter 4.

Part II focuses on improvement of productivity and quality by presenting a variety of models of factors and their relationships. Chapter 5 explains four general descriptive models to help the reader gain an understanding of the conceptualization of the problem and the many complex interactions involved. The models in Chapter 6 are prescriptive as well as descriptive and lead to more specific suggestions for improvement methods.

Part III ties together measurement with improvement. Chapter 7 presents conclusions from the several research studies cited and makes recommendations for practical applications of the models and measurement techniques.

PART I
MEASURING THE QUALITY DIMENSION OF PRODUCTIVITY

AN APPROACH TO MEASUREMENT

The primary thrust of this book is the quality dimension of productivity. What type of measurement problem should be anticipated? What type of data exists or can be collected?

The traditional economic and engineering view of productivity as a ratio of outputs to inputs reflects the economic and engineering efficiency concept. Quality, frequently discussed as effectiveness, often receives an emphasis secondary to productivity. Within some functions and organizations we perceive a parallel emphasis of traditional productivity and quality, but infrequently does a quality emphasis truly dominate productivity. One reason for not emphasizing quality is that it is difficult to measure--especially in service departments or organizations.

We are suggesting in this part of this book that quality can be measured in the same output-to-input conceptual framework as can traditional productivity or efficiency. If this can be done, one of the barriers to a quality emphasis in organizations--the barrier of quality measurement--can be laid aside. The organization can strive for productivity improvements on a broader basis if quality can be identified and measured similarly to quantity.

Several questions guided our initial investigation. What type of measurement problem should be anticipated? What type of data exists or can be collected? How well is quality actually defined for processes, especially in service departments? The data scaling issue, for example, was addressed early in the project as illustrated in the next paragraph.

At the lowest level in organizations, where individual and small-group performance quality is being measured, interval and ratio scaled data can be collected. For example, the number of errors that a bank teller makes in cash reconciliation in one day is a quality dimension measurable on a ratio scale. At levels in the organization above the operative level, administrators are normally held responsible for grouped individual performances of first-line workers. Group performance often will be interval or ratio scaled data, such as percentage defective in a department or department rework costs. However, when a service or administrative environment is substituted for a manufacturing, product-oriented environment, individual and group performances must generally be measured more subjectively. It becomes more difficult to identify and measure product attributes. Therefore, definition of output variables in associated measurement is less rigorous. It is not unusual when measuring service function quality at the organization level to find nominal or ordinal data.

Judging from the quality and productivity literature, the measurement problem is understood to be one of measuring (1) technology, (2) psychological or sociological dimensions of work, and (3) economic performance variables. Any measurement scheme developed should have the flexibility to measure the combination of technological, behavioral, and economic variables that clearly affect the quality dimension of productivity.

MEASURING QUALITY

Quality is measured in a manufacturing product environment either by attributes or by variables. Attributes measurement involves those characteristics of the product that make it either "good" or "bad." Scratches on an aluminum refrigerator shelf molding would be judged as either good (acceptable) or bad (unacceptable) depending upon the general appearance of the finish. Measurement by variables infers that product characteristics are measurable on a variable or ratio scale. Examples are temperature, length, density, and diameter. Product attribute characteristics lend themselves to analysis using the binominal distribution; variable characteristics lend themselves to measurement by a wider range of probability distributions.

In services, one thinks of measurement for the total service organization (such as an insurance company, a university, or a municipality) or for the service function within an organization (computer services, personnel services, and accounting services). There is no product to be measured--only the service output. Services generally are not stored; they are consumed upon generation. At times the producer of the service is, in fact, the actual consumer. For example, in cafeterias customers are involved in walking their trays through the line and often carrying them back to tables where the food is consumed. Thus the customers are partially involved in the generation of food service. These service characteristics make measurement much more difficult; the service generated is more intangible.

There can be, and is, measurement by attribute similar to measurement in manufacturing. The service can be judged qualitatively as good or bad. Specific measurement by variable is much more difficult. Quality is measured primarily by consumer complaints, the attitudes of consumers, observation, or the subjective assessment of the producer. Typically, formal methods for measuring service quality do not exist. In motels and hotels generally a form is somewhere about the room or facility that solicits voluntary service evaluation. That form plus casual observation comprise the quality audit. Less typically, but utilized in some chains such as Marriott (Hostage 1975), a quality audit of services is performed on a periodic basis. In summary, the measurement problem for measuring performance quality is substantially more difficult in services than in manufacturing.

MEASURING THE QUALITY DIMENSION OF PRODUCTIVITY

In measuring the quality dimension of productivity, several requirements must be met. First, due to the nature of the productivity ratio, both inputs and outputs must be measured. Organizations tend to develop measures for outputs more readily than they do for inputs. Very few cases were found in which inputs were measured, and there were even fewer in which the quality dimension of inputs were measured and subsequently related to outputs. A second requirement is that technology, group behavioral factors, and economic variables must all be measured.

Consistent with the productivity measurement literature reviewed and quality measurement difficulties in service industries and service functions, a descriptive approach to measurement was anticipated. The approach required development of an explicative procedure in which data were based on nominal or classificatory scaled data. Some ordinal or ranking scale data might exist, but very little, if any, ratio scale data were expected (Siegal 1956, pp. 21-30).

Chapter 3, A Measure-Development Procedure, presents the quality-measurement procedure developed for services. In applying and presenting this procedure in seminars, we have found a need for early presentation of example quality measures--the result of the measurement procedure. This is the purpose of Chapter 2. Chapter 4 will present details of the first applications of the quality-measurement procedure.

2

Productivity Measures for Quality

Although the primary purpose of this book is to present the development of an approach to measuring the quality dimension of productivity, in this chapter we want to digress from that theme somewhat. In explaining quality as a productivity concept to business and government leaders and in applying the measurement approach in organizations, we have become aware of the confusion that the measurement procedure terminology introduces, frequently masking the simplicity of quality measures. Executives and participants in the procedure seem to benefit from an early presentation of example measures, followed by the procedure for obtaining the measures. Therefore, in this chapter we will present quality measures, quality indicators, and quality-productivity ratios, as illustrations of both the state of the art and possible improvements in quality measurement. In Chapter 3 we will return to the measure development procedure.

THE CURRENT STATE OF THE ART IN MEASURING QUALITY IN SERVICES: TWO ILLUSTRATIONS FROM COMMERCIAL BANKING

First National Bank of Atlanta

First National Bank of Atlanta is a leading bank in the Southeastern United States with over 2,200 employees, 1,110 of whom are in operations, and with \$3.0 billion of assets and \$2.1 billion of deposits.[1] This places First National of Atlanta as the 68th largest commercial bank in the United States.[2]

First National Bank of Atlanta is a regional processor for many national accounts, including major consumer credit activities such as VISA, and enjoys a reputation of quality services to customers. The bank has developed a quality control report for systemwide operations. A page from this monthly report appears in Figure 2-1.

Interpreting the report, which is for February, 1980, we see three measures being recorded for the bookkeeping department relating to customer service by telephone. The measures for the first two graphs concern lost calls and represent a percentage answered (percentage good quality). Lost calls are defined as calls that were logged on the telephone systems but were not answered before the caller terminated the call. For each of these two charts, below the dashed line at 90% represents the out-of-control or poor-quality area, from the middle dashed horizontal line to the dashed line represents a warning zone area of potential poor quality, and the top solid horizontal line, the 1980 management goal of 95%. The histories for 1979 and 1980 are represented by dashed and solid lines, respectively. The third graph simply plots total busy signals. The busy signals reflect overflow recorded by the telephone system and would appear to be as much related to capacity planning and manpower staffing as to quality. One could view overflow as a source of customer-perceived poor service rather than an error source.

These graphs are typical of useful quality error measures and indicators. First National Bank of Atlanta has a fairly complete set of such measures, and managers

---

[1]The authors would like to acknowledge Thomas G. Goodrum and The First National Bank of Atlanta for their willingness to share quality procedures and results.

[2]There are approximately 14,700 commercial banks in the United States in 1980.

Figure 2-1a

First National Bank of Atlanta Quality Report

Subject: 7111--External Customer Service
Division: Account Administration
Error: Lost Call
Source: Bookkeeping

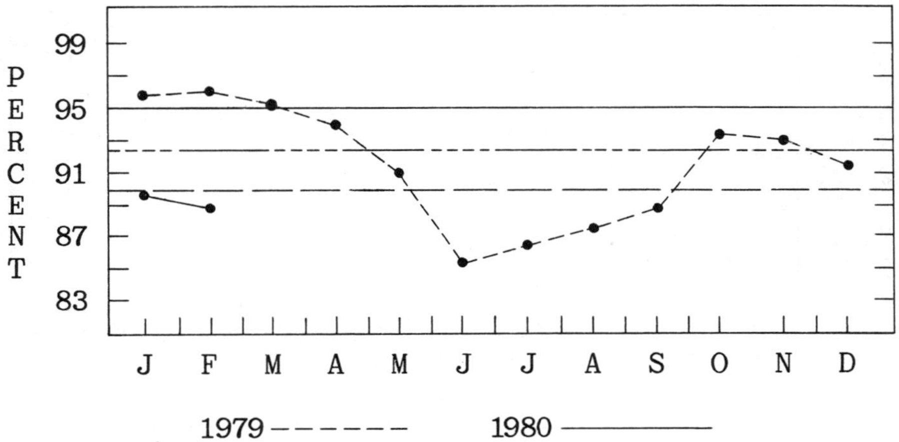

	January	February	December '79
Total incoming calls	39,997	18,151*	32,293
Total calls answered	35,906	16,152*	29,427
Total lost calls	4,091	1,999*	2,866
Percentage answered	89.8%	89.0%	91.1%
Goal	95.0%	95.0%	95.0%

The percentage of customer service calls logged on the phone system that were answered (does not include calls that received a busy signal)

*Data reflect only the first two weeks of February; during the last two weeks, the new phone system was being installed.

Figure 2-1b

First National Bank of Atlanta Quality Report

Subject: 7378--Internal Customer Service
Division: Account Administration
Error: Lost Call
Source: Bookkeeping

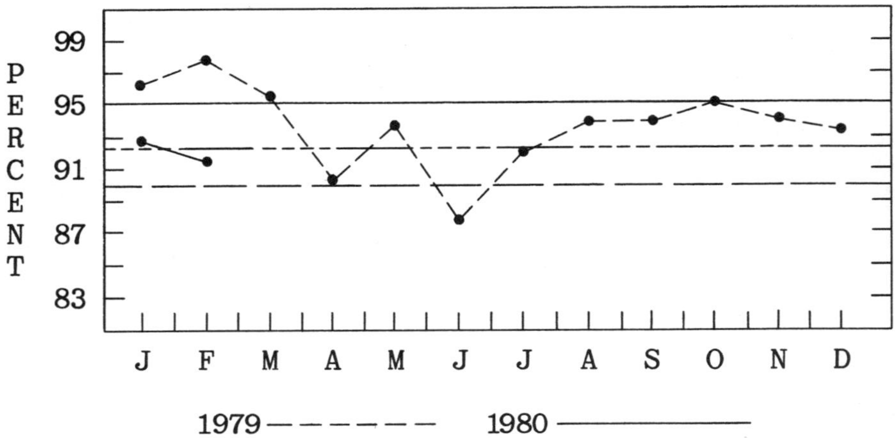

	January	February	December '79
Total incoming calls	27,374	11,868*	23,273
Total calls answered	25,413	10,856*	21,791
Total lost calls	1,961	1,012*	1,482
Percentage answered	92.8%	91.5%	93.6%
Goal	95.0%	95.0%	95.0%

The percentage of customer service calls logged on the phone system that were answered (does not include calls that received a busy signal)

*Data reflect only the first two weeks of February; during the last two weeks, the new phone system was being installed.

Figure 2-1c

First National Bank of Atlanta Quality Report

Subject: Customer Service
Division: Account Administration
Error: Busy Signal (overflow)
Source: Bookkeeping

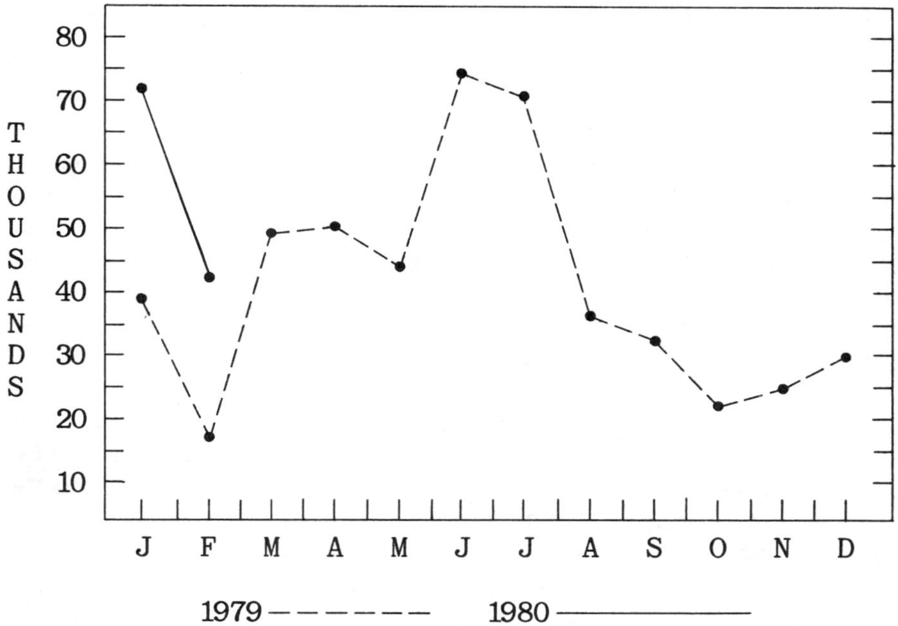

	January	February	December '79
Busy signals, external	61,684	25,665*	15,344
Busy signals, internal	42,933	17,807*	14,883
Total busy signals	104,617	43,472*	30,227

The total number of busy signals (overflow) recorded by the phone system in Bookkeeping Customer Service (internal and external sections).

*Data reflect only the first two weeks of February; during the last two weeks, the new phone system was being installed.

look at each separately for various organization units. Notice that sampling and formal control charts were not used in this application. Managers control costs for the bookeeping department from traditional managerial accounting records--examining budget variances and standard cost reports. Quality and costs for maintaining a given level of quality are not combined in one ratio or report. Based on our observations in work with quality experts in many commercial banks, this is representative of current quality control procedures in banking.

Northwestern National Bank of Minneapolis

Northwestern National Bank of Minneapolis enjoys a reputation in banking of having developed rather complete quality measures throughout the bank.[3] This leading bank has over 2,100 employees, 700 of whom are in operations. Assets total $3.8 billion and deposits are $2.7 billion. This ranks Northwestern National as 50th among the largest commercial banks.

Organizationally, Northwestern National groups the staff functions of productivity analysis and quality control together into a Productivity and Quality Analysis Section. The quality control subgroup's objective is to assist managers in early detection of potential quality problem situations and timely reaction to these situations before they develop to crisis proportions.

Our intent in this chapter is to focus on measurement; several interesting points concerning Northwestern National Bank's quality program will be discussed later in the book. Figure 2-2 presents a sample quality analysis source report for the proof section during May 1979.

Northwestern National has developed a quality control training manual, a portion of which is devoted to explaining and interpreting the standardized quality analysis source report. Essentially, the focus

---

[3]The authors would like to acknowledge Victor A. Schwinghamer, quality control officer, and Northwestern National Bank of Minneapolis for their willingness to share quality procedures and results.

Figure 2-2

Northwestern National Bank of Minneapolis Quality Report

SOURCE: PROOF SECTION   QUALITY ANALYSIS SOURCE REPORT   MONTH: MAY, 1979

Defect/Control Subject	This Month's Error Ratio	Percent Defective			Quality Standard	% Deviation from Standard
		May	April	March		
Credit TC errors/ total items processed	850 /7598632	.011	.008	.009	.010	-25.0
X Items rejected/ total items processed	81305/7598632	1.070	.998	1.201	1.200	17.5
X Proof differences/ total items processed	1452 /7598632	.019	.017	.015	.016	-75.0
+ Defective $ amount field/ total items processed	31256/7598632	.411	.467	.532	.500	29.7
Defecive trancode field/ total items processed	5153 /7598632	.068	.071	.062	.100	64.0
Terminations this month/ full time employees	2 /35	5.714*	2.857	0.	2.500	-100.0
Terminations this month/ part time employees	3 /85	3.529	4.706	1.118	5.000	49.0

Defects--Error Ratio Not Applicable	Defect Volume			Quality Standard	% Deviation from Standard
	May	April	March		
+ Out of balance internal entries-- average/week	30	42*	51*	120	-50.0
Error correction notices written-- average/week	1015	987	993	950	-43.3
Proof operators force balance-- total/month	11	6	9	15	10.0
Cash ticket errors--total/week	375	422	298	400	12.5
Extra items at end of day--average/day	4*	15	8	12	100.0
+ Adjustments required on proof activity-- total/month	175	256	375*	200	25.0

Net Deviation = 14.4%; Number of Measures = 13; Q.C.I. Score = 1.1%

```
***** KEY *****                       % DEVI-
* :Process out of control              ATION
+ :Pyramided to division report       - 40 -                                                     -
X :Pyramided to dept. report          - 30 -                                                     -
% Deviation from std.: reflects       - 20 - *                                                   -
  position within control zone        - 10 -    *  *                                             -
 Net deviation: mathematical             0 - -  -  -  -  -  -  -  -  -  -  -  *  *-
  summation of all deviations           10 -          *           *  *                           -
 Q.C.I. score (quality composite        20 -             *  *     *        *                     -
  index): net deviations divided        30 -                   *                                 -
  by number of subjects--re-            40 - .  .  .  .  .  .  .  .  .  .  .  .  .-
  flects ability to meet stan-               M  J  J  A  S  O  N  D  J  F  M  A  M
  dards (should be near "0%")                78                                   79
```

statistic is the percentage of deviation from standard in the far right-hand column. Note that the first 7 of the 13 measures shown in the printout focus on percentage defective, whereas the lower portion of the printout focuses on volumes defective. After all 13 measures are converted to percentage deviation from standard, they are averaged. This average, the quality composite index (QCI), is plotted. A positive QCI is a positive variance from standard--a composite quality level that is better than standard (that has fewer errors than standard).

One of the key features of this reporting system is the potential to pyramid quality reports. Sections can be averaged for division quality reports and divisions pyramided through averaging for an overall organization composite quality index.

Underlying the approach of Northwestern National is an assumption that all quality measures--the hundreds throughout the bank--are of equal importance. One might want to use a weighting scheme to reduce or eliminate many of the measures as pyramiding takes place.

Northwestern National Bank also uses control charts in operations for selected quality measures. These are used at critical quality variance points in processes. In summary, the quality reporting system of this bank is one of the best that we have observed, comparing favorably with that of the Federal Reserve banking system in both scope and accuracy.

A common omission in these two examples and in the measurement of quality in most service organizations is that performance measures are not related to resources consumed. Putting quality performance into output-to-input ratios would focus managerial concern on both the effectiveness and the efficiency of quality programs and actions. Even in manufacturing firms well known for quality, we have frequently heard concern for not knowing "if we spend too much money and effort on our quality image." This suggests that manufacturing firms have also failed to develop measures for quality productivity. The next section develops the concept of quality-productivity ratios. Such ratios can be developed for either services or products.

QUALITY-PRODUCTIVITY RATIOS

A comprehensive statement of the QPR would be

$$QPR_1 = \frac{\text{Number of items not rejected}}{\begin{bmatrix}\text{Total number of items} \times \text{Processing cost per item}\end{bmatrix} + \begin{bmatrix}\text{Number of error items} \times \text{Reject (error) processing cost per item}\end{bmatrix}} \quad (2\text{-}1)$$

This ratio allows for changes in quantity by allowing the ratio to react to quality changes in the numerator yet being sensitive to volume changes in the denominator. A quality penalty cost, such as lost resources, could be added as another cost item in the denominator if it were appropriate.

It is implied in this ratio that each rejected item (error) is processed again, i.e., corrected at some unit cost, and eventually becomes a "good" item. This would be the common case for many service items. For products, however, the economics of correction might suggest scrapping the product rather than correcting it. If that were so, the quality-productivity ratio above (equation 2-1) would require adjustment. In the denominator the number of error items being corrected would be less than all items rejected, as scrapped items are not reworked. One might also argue that a negative term should be added to the denominator, reflecting the salvage value of scrap, i.e., subtract the number of items scrapped times the unit salvage value. This reflects a reduction in the resources required to give the output quality of the numerator.

An alternative statement of the QPR would be

$$QPR_2 = \frac{\text{Number of items not rejected}}{\text{Total number of items} \times \text{Processing cost per item}} \quad (2\text{-}2)$$

This ratio ignores the cost of reprocessing errors. One argument for this ratio is that, in most service functions, all items are eventually processed as good units; therefore the processing cost per item can be a unit cost that includes error corrections. Clearly, the simplified form is attractive.

Yet another statement of the QPR is

$$QPR_3 = \frac{\text{Number of items not rejected}}{\text{Number of error items} \times \text{Reject (error) processing cost per item}} \quad (2\text{-}3)$$

This ratio relates the good pieces to the cost of correcting pieces that are not good. Proponents of this ratio might argue that good pieces over correction costs focuses on quality throughout and does not allow total processing costs to mask quality performance.

Overall, the first ratio, QPR_1, most closely represents the concept of productivity--the ratio of output to the resources required to produce that output. The output in terms of quality is good items; the resources are the sum of resources required to initially produce the good and bad items plus the resources required to transform the items from bad to good.

Example Ratios

The first quality productivity ratio (2-1) will be utilized throughout the following examples and referred to as QPR.

Example 1. Consider a simple case of 100 items produced in a time period, 90 of which are good and 10 of which are rejected. The processing costs are \$100/1,000 items, and the error (reject) correction costs are \$1,000/1,000 items.

1-A. What is the QPR?

$$QPR = \frac{\text{Number good}}{\left[\text{Number processed} \times \text{Cost to process}\right] + \left[\text{Number rejected} \times \text{Cost to correct reject}\right]}$$

$$= \frac{90}{100(\$.10) + 10(\$1.00)} = \frac{90}{20} = 4.5 \text{ units per dollar}$$

1-B. What is the impact of doubling volume on the QPR? Now 180 are good, and 20 are rejected.

$$QPR = \frac{180}{200(\$.10) + 20(\$1.00)} = \frac{180}{40} = 4.5 \text{ units per dollar}$$

There is no change in QPR.

1-C. What is the impact of decreasing processing cost on the QPR? Let the processing cost decrease from \$100/1,000 to \$90/1,000 items.

$$QPR = \frac{90}{100(\$.09) + 10(\$1.00)} = \frac{90}{19} = 4.73 \text{ units per dollar}$$

The QPR increased. The same good pieces for fewer dollars of resources should drive the QPR up. That is what happened.

1-D. What is the impact of error (reject) correction costs decreasing? Let the cost of error correction decrease from \$1,000/1,000 to \$900/1,000 items.

$$QPR = \frac{90}{100(\$.10) + 10(\$.09)} = \frac{90}{19} = 4.73 \text{ units per dollar}$$

The QPR increased. If error correction costs decrease, then QPR should increase; that was illustrated to be so.

1-E. What is the impact of more good pieces being produced? Let 95 pieces be good, with 5 rejected.

$$QPR = \frac{95}{100(\$.10) + 5(\$1.00)} = \frac{95}{15} = 6.33 \text{ units per dollar}$$

The QPR increased, as logically it should.

1-F. What is the impact of more bad pieces being produced? Let 85 pieces be good, with 15 rejected.

$$QPR = \frac{85}{100(\$.10) + 15(\$1.00)} = \frac{85}{25} = 3.4 \text{ units per dollar}$$

The QPR declined as more items were rejected within the same cost structure. Logically, that would be desirable for a quality-productivity ratio.

Example 2. Bank X has the largest lock box operation in its market area and is interested in developing one quality-productivity ratio to measure operating performance on a quality dimension. Management is interested in a ratio that relates quality produced to the resources being consumed to produce that quality level. The following data for December 1978 exist.

Total customer-reported errors	312
Total number of payments processed	605,721
Average transaction cost (previous month's total direct operating expense for function divided by total volume)	$0.150
Average transaction cost to process customer-reported error (a 1977 standard cost)	$0.451

Calculating the QPR,

$$\text{QPR} = \frac{(605{,}721 - 312)}{605{,}721(\$.15) + 312(\$.451)}$$

$$= \frac{605{,}409}{\$90{,}858.15 + \$140.71} = \frac{605{,}409}{\$90{,}998.86}$$

$$= 6.65 \text{ transactions per dollar}$$

Example 3. Savings and Loan Association Y is a competitor of Bank X. Savings and Loan Y has a money transfer operation that seems quite efficient to management. Although management has information on total errors in money transfer, quality has never been related formally to costs. The following data were collected so that a quality-productivity ratio could be constructed.

Total of any errors in money transfer	4
Total number of money transfers	24,168
Total processing cost per transaction (November's total direct operating expense for Money Transfer Dept. divided by total number of money transfers)	$1.40
Average transaction cost to correct and process a money transfer error (average cost for errors in November)	$10.00
Average dollar claims paid and dollar interest lost per money transfer error (September penalty charges against department per number of errors in September)	Data not available

Calculating the QPR,

$$QPR = \frac{(24,168 - 64)}{(24,168)(\$1.40) + 64(\$10.00 + \$N/A)}$$

$$= 0.699 \text{ transfers per dollar}$$

Example 4. Savings and Loan Association Y management believes that a good quality indicator for money transfer is the number of missed deadlines. The following data for missed deadlines were collected and corrective action is under consideration at the present time.

Month	Number of Missed Deadlines
June	3
July	2
August	4
September	8
October	12
November	11

Missed deadlines can be considered a "quality indicator" and should not be ignored simply because they are not expressed as a QPR. Many quality indicators are meaningful to managers.

Interpretation of Ratios

The following example is intended to illustrate how quality-productivity ratios can be traced over time.

Example 5. Bank X (see Example 2) has reconstructed quality-productivity ratios for 1980 as shown in Figure 2-3.

After examining the QPR trend, volumes and customer-reported errors were analyzed. These had not changed drastically (see Table 2-1). The August-November quality productivity gain was not explained by number of errors or volume. Management found that in recent months processing costs per transaction were dropping because fewer personnel were being used. Quality (number of good pieces) was being held constant, outputs were constant, but fewer people were doing the work. Equal quality with less resources resulted in a quality-productivity ratio increase for August-November.

Figure 2-3

Lock Box Quality

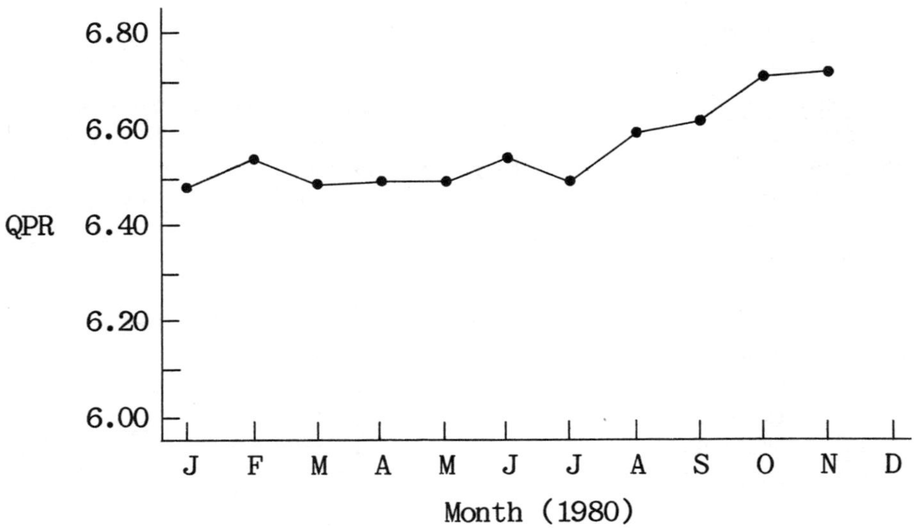

Table 2-1

Bank X Lock Box Errors and Volume

Month	Lock Box Customer-Reported Errors	Lock Box Total Payments Processed	% Error
January	295	580,014	.051%
February	312	601,110	.052
March	287	575,911	.050
April	268	571,421	.047
May	297	607,314	.049
June	305	610,511	.050
July	307	591,112	.052
August	269	574,110	.047
September	311	586,797	.053
October	336	611,411	.055
November	311	598,791	.052
December	312	605,721	.051

DEVELOPMENT OF QPR SETS

In applying a measure-development process (to be explained in Chapter 3) to a specific organization or department, we found that a set of ratios and quality indicators is necessary. Productivity is not a unidimensional construct; the myriad of performance characteristics and social and technical resources involved in producing a service are best evaluated by a set of ratios rather than by a single weighted index. This is particularly true if the measurement focuses on productivity improvement. Ratios related to specific input factors allow an organization to monitor the effect of changes in managerial strategy and actions. A single index masks the effects of intervening managerial decisions.

Table 2-2 displays a set of measures developed for the office-processing tasks of Federal Reserve bank personnel departments. Notice that four different performance characteristics are reflected in the four measures and that five unique types of costs are used in the denominators. Three of the measures also demonstrate the concept of timeliness as a quality dimension. The success in including the several aspects of quality productivity in the set of measures is enhanced by the inclusion of a diagonal cross section of personnel staff in measure development.

One issue that always arises as we discuss such measures with service managers is the practicality of gathering the data for ratios. The two examples of current measurement practice given early in this chapter illustrate that many organizations gather the needed performance data. Other performance data, such as the number of personnel files current and free of errors (measure 3 in Table 2-2), can be obtained rather easily by application of sampling plans that have been used for years in monitoring manufacturing functions. Examining all personnel files to obtain a measure would obviously be prohibitive to gathering the needed data; pulling only a small percentage of the files on a random sampling basis is certainly a more reasonable alternative. Other needed data, such as the nature of how requests are handled, may be obtained by the simple addition of a few boxes to check off on the request form. Cost data

Table 2-2

Measures for Office Processing

Numerator	Denominator
1. Number of required external and top-level information requests satisfactorily processed within standard or requested time period	(Number of requests x average cost per request) + (Number of clarifications required x cost per clarification)
2. Number of employee benefit and information requests handled satisfactorily and within timelines	(Number of requests x cost per request) + (number of corrections requested x cost per correction)
3. Number of personnel files current and free of errors	(Number of employees x cost per file) + (number of corrections requested x cost per correction)
4. Number of personnel files for new employees correctly processed within a standard time limit	(Number of new employees x cost to create a new employee file) + (number of errors detected x cost per error corrected)

may be obtained by work sampling, averaging total time to process a set of items, time and motion standards, periodic audits, or the addition of data collection to existing forms.

Developing sets of measures for service-related groups, such as a methods analysis department, is not really more difficult, but more use of quality "indicators" may be required. Examples of quality indicators and ratios for a project environment are given in Table 2-3. Notice that several of the indicators reflect time spent on quality difficulties and customer response to quality "image."

Table 2-3

Measures for Methods Project Function

Numerator	Denominator
1. Percentage of projects not receiving negative feedback	
2. Number of rewrite hours	Total project hours
3. Number of follow-up projects	Total original projects
4. Percentage of requests with conflicting or confusing objectives	
5. Number of weeks between report presentation and request implementation	
The measures preceding are indicators; those following are QPRs.	
6. Number of project specifications not requiring change	(Cost to set each spec) x (number of specs)
7. Number of projects with satisfactory and timely documentation	Cost of documenting a project x number of projects) + (cost to rework documentation x number requiring revision of documents)
8. Number of recommendations accepted by requesting departments	(Cost to prepare a recommendation x number of specific recommendations) + (cost to revise recommendation x number of revisions attempted)

SUMMARY

Productivity measurement for quality can be expressed in terms of a ratio reflecting the numerator (outputs) as good items and the denominator (inputs) as a combination of the resources required to produce the item and the resources required for error correction. Two examples of contemporary quality measurement were presented from banking; neither one uses this quality-productivity ratio concept. After a presentation of examples of quality-productivity ratios, two example applications were presented from personnel services and methods analysis services. Details of the procedure for developing the productivity ratios will be discussed in the next chapter.

3
A Measure Development Procedure

A PROTOTYPICAL APPROACH

Hopefully, you are now curious about the source of the numerous quality-productivity ratios that were presented in the previous chapter. Were they developed based upon our knowledge of current management theory? Were they gleaned from a survey of numerous research projects on quality measurement in services? Were they obtained by surveying leading productivity measurement experts? Were they found by asking managers of service functions what they are currently doing to measure quality? Were they set by experts outside the firm? Quite to the contrary, these ratios were developed by employees within the organization who are not productivity experts.

Quality-productivity ratios for service firms or functions can be developed by nearly anyone by following a short, simple, robust procedure for gathering, shaping, and combining the basic knowledge that those who work with a service already have. Drawing from theories and experiences in operations management, sociotechnical systems, structured group processes, quality control, and productivity measurement, a procedure has been developed, tested, revised, and successfully implemented that provides quality-productivity ratios for any service group.

This chapter presents the steps in this prototypical procedure. Although the step-by-step narrative can become a bit tedious to read, actually conducting the steps is rather simple and straighforward. Throughout the chapter a simple example is used from a commercial laundry. Productivity measures are ultimately developed in this example for laundering a shirt. We caution the reader to keep the measurement procedure separate from the laundry example. The thrust of this chapter is to present the quality-measurement procedure, and the laundry example is woven into the discussion as a simple, clarifying example.

ASSUMPTIONS AND PREREQUISITES

Some important ingredients of the prototypical approach should be kept in mind through this discussion:

1. The approach provides a framework for creating a unique set of measures for each service and each organization to which it is applied.

2. It assumes that the knowledge needed to create a measurement system exists within the minds of current system managers.

3. Structured group procedures used throughout are vital to creating an appropriate atmosphere of openness and creative thought.

4. Productivity is considered a multidimensional construct and thus should be measured by sets of related measures rather than by a single index number.

5. The approach should be attempted only with strong top management support in assuring that all needed personnel can be made available without interruptions during group sessions.

Throughout explanation of the approach, handouts and examples to be used are presented. To follow the example, it is assumed that the general nature of shirt laundering either is known already or is transparent. Assume that no other services are available from the firm. There is no need to make statements about factors such as size, ownership, equipment, and location, as such factors are immaterial in the use of the example.

AN OVERVIEW OF THE QUALITY MEASUREMENT PROCEDURE

Table 3-1 provides an overview of the prototypical measurement procedure, identifying all activities. There is considerable flexibility in group content and the role of the project coordinators. Any modification should retain the basic procedure, which involves establishing system boundaries, identifying unit operations, generating key quality deviations, generating quality measures, and ranking the quality measures. Details of this approach follow.

Table 3-1

Measurement Procedure Activities

Activity Sequence	Activity
1	Decide to measure productivity (top management)
2	Select project coordinators
3	Become familiar with system
4	Select participants; divide into groups
5	Define system and establish boundaries
6	Determine unit operations
7	Generate, select, and rank deviations
8	Determine final key quality deviations
9	Generate key quality deviation measures
10	Collect technology and systems input data
11	Edit measures into productivity ratios
12	Clarify edited measures and revise as necessary
13	Put measures into questionnaire format
14	Rank productivity measures by completing questionnaire
15	Evaluate questionnaire results and produce final quality-productivity ratios

PROJECT COORDINATOR SELECTION

Once top management has committed itself to productivity measurement, project coordinators must be selected. The development of the measurement system is coordinated by two individuals who are familiar with the function to be analyzed and the special terminology used within the system. These two coordinators must not currently belong to the group being analyzed. They may be from another area of the organization with prior experience in the function under consideration or they may be staff analysts who have studied the function previously. Two individuals are needed to help avoid the introduction of researcher bias. The two coordinators can police the neutrality of each other's comments and actions. Two people are also needed for interactive development and group sessions during some phases of the project. Substantial decreases in elapsed calendar time will result from using two coordinators rather than one. An additional benefit from the use of two coordinators is the opportunity for a coordinator experienced in the technique to teach an inexperienced coordinator. There should be no observers during the project.

Project coordinators should already possess skills in leading group discussions and decision making and in understanding the function under analysis and its terminology. Skills to be gained before conducting the project include understanding of productivity and productivity measures and understanding of the nominal group process. The two coordinators should have run at least one nominal group session with an unrelated group prior to the project. Outside help on productivity and the process may be useful; however, careful reading of this book and close adherence to the steps described in this chapter have proved to be adequate for successful implementation.

FAMILIARIZATION WITH SYSTEM

The coordinators begin the project by becoming familiar with the details of the organization and system. The first step is to obtain organizational data such as (1) structure charts with names and position titles for all supervisors and managers, (2) job descriptions, (3) sample reports and their distribution, (4) statements on policies, goals, and objectives, and (5) any previous special managerial studies on the system. The second step is to obtain technology information such as (1) flow charts and layout diagrams, (2) equipment and technology investment studies, and (3) plans for future technology developments and changes. The third step is to visit the system site for a one-day overview. An extensive tour of the physical facility should be made followed by brief interviews with a vertical cross section of the system and the managerial levels above the system.

PARTICIPANT SELECTION

Since the procedure primarily involves determination by system management, it is important to form the groups correctly. Two groups comprising a vertical cross section of the system's management are needed. Group A includes the manager immediately above the top level included in the system, the top manager within system boundaries, and representatives from managerial levels below the top system manager down to, but not including, the managers responsible for conducting daily or weekly operations. Group B includes representatives of all managerial levels and staff groups from first-line supervision up through the managers responsible for daily or weekly operations.

Group A may range in size from two to five individuals. Group B may range in size from six to ten, with the combined number of people in the two groups not exceeding twelve. It is important that key people in actual delivery of the service be members of the teams. It is also useful to have a mix of individuals with a variety of backgrounds and length of service.

SYSTEM DEFINITION AND BOUNDARIES

Based upon the system background information, the two coordinators define the system and its boundaries. Demand for the services of the system is determined by identifying the location at which the customer interacts

Figure 3-1

System Boundaries: Shirt Laundry Operation

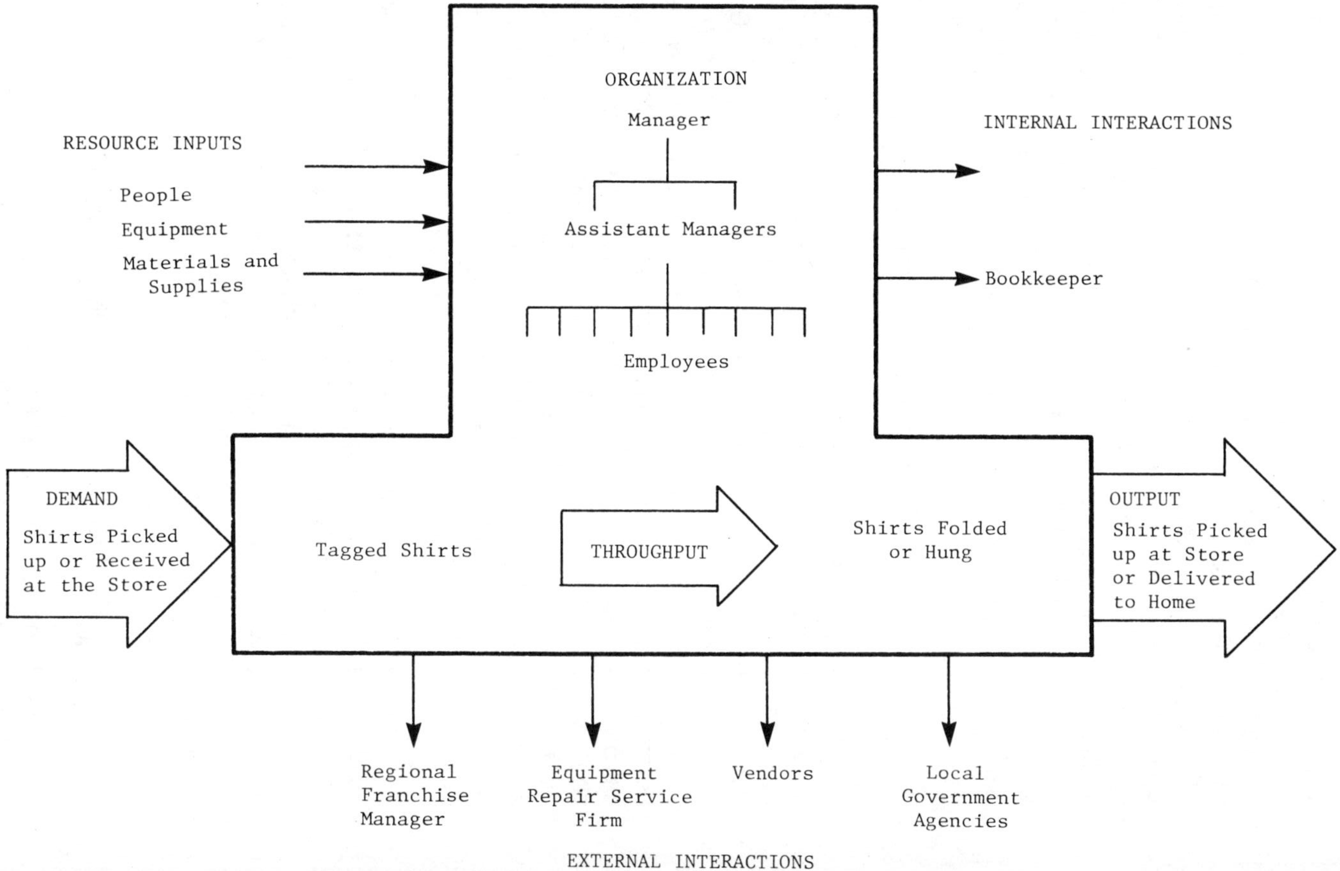

with the system and the nature of the demand request. Output definition requires customer identification and determination of both the timing and location of delivery of the services. Establishing physical and social boundaries requires decisions about (1) the top level of management to be included within the system, (2) functional groups to be included in the system, (3) physical plant and equipment included within the system, (4) major internal groups and managers interacting with the system, and (5) major external groups interacting with the system. Types of input needed to transform demand to outputs include (1) people, (2) equipment, (3) materials and supplies, and (4) support systems. Definition of the system and its boundaries yields a diagram of the system to be analyzed. Figure 3-1 outlines the shirt laundering system.

GROUP SESSIONS

A series of group meetings is conducted over a three-day period to determine deviations in the throughput of the system. A deviation is a difference from norm or standard for a technical requirement of the system. At no time are examples for the current system allowed.

Session 1: Purpose, Terminology, and Approval of System Boundaries

The first session is to introduce the project, explain concepts and terminology to be used, and finalize system boundaries. Both groups A and B attend this session. Introduction of the project involves explanation of who initiated the project and why, credentials of project coordinators, general steps to be followed and timing, results expected, and planned use of results. Explanation of concepts and terminology requires a discussion of sociotechnical systems primarily. Systems are explained in relation to the diagram presented in Figure 3-2. A system is described in terms of these characteristics: (1) set of parts and subsystems, (2) interrelated parts, (3) organized set, (4) goal-directed set, and (5) set with properties unique to whole. It is explained that system boundaries can be defined in terms of people, territories, technologies, and time. The

Figure 3–2

Sociotechnical System Elements

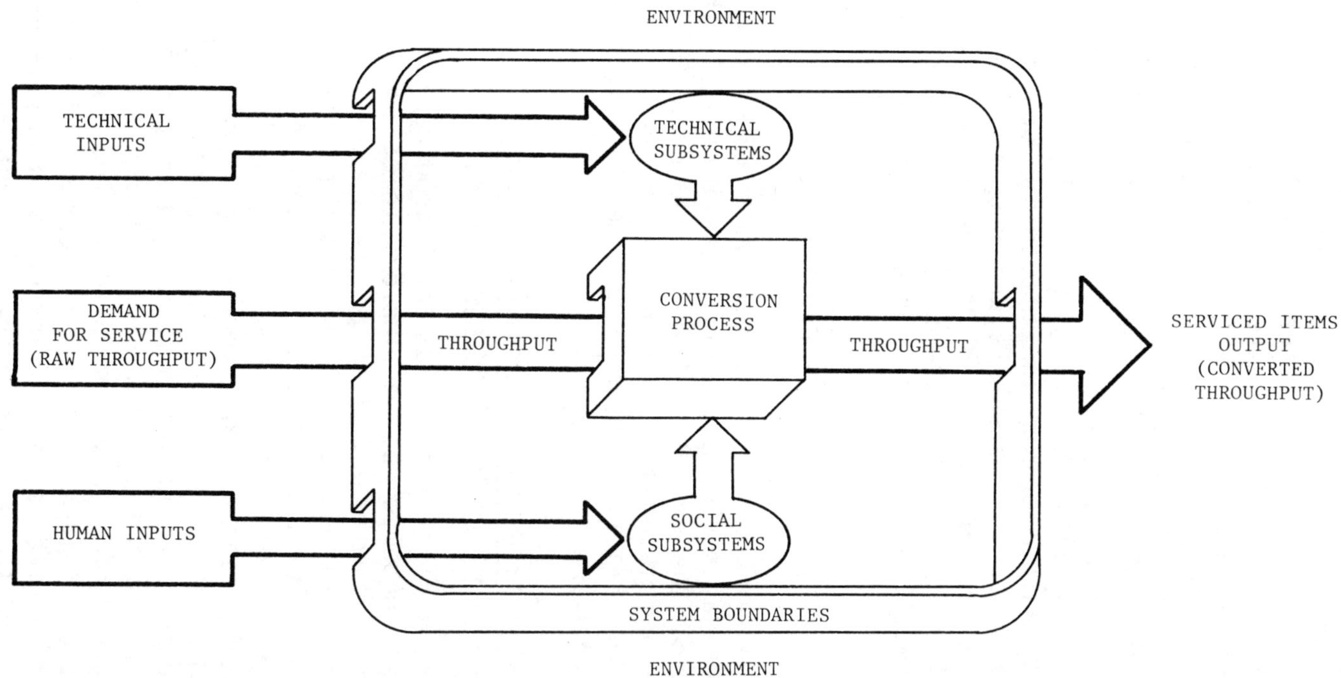

components of systems shown in Figure 3-2 are then covered. The following statement can be used to clarify system components:

> The focal point in looking at an organizational function as a sociotechnical system is on the throughput. Throughput refers to the demand for service to the conversion process, changes in the state of the throughput during the conversion process, and a modified throughput as some expected serviced output. The state changes required in the throughput may be obtained with any of a large number of combinations of technical systems (capital) and social systems (labor), but the same basic series of state changes will be required regardless of which particular combination is chosen.

Following time for questions concerning system concepts, the diagram of the system to be analyzed is presented and explained. Revisions are subjected to group discussion and then finalized according to group wishes.

The final topic to be explained is a unit operation. A unit operation refers to any one of the phases in a system in which an identifiable state change in the throughput occurs. Figure 3-3 is the handout used to clarify the concept. The state changes for shirt laundering are then discussed as an example of unit operations. The unit operations are (1) receive and tag, (2) wash and clean, (3) dry and press, and (4) package and deliver. Shirts are the throughput. Questions from the group should be directed toward the laundry illustration to avoid bias for the function under analysis.

This first group session is then closed with a quick summary of the steps to be followed. The meeting should last about one hour.

Session 2: Establishing Unit Operations

Immediately following the project introduction meeting, group B only is convened for about 15 minutes to begin establishment of unit operations for the system

Figure 3-3

Handout on Unit Operations

UNIT OPERATIONS

CHARACTERISTICS

1. Unit operations refers to any one of the phases in a system in which an identifiable state change in the throughput occurs.

2. Defining unit operations requires that you analyze the system in terms of the state changes to the throughput.

3. Each unit operation describes a different transformation to the demand for service item that does not overlap with the other unit operations.

NUMBER OF UNIT OPERATIONS

You can probably establish fewer unit operations for the system than you think at first.

1. This is because many of the operations or tasks performed on the throughput are control, checking, verification, or inspection activities rather than fundamental changes in the throughput items.

2. Also, several tasks, jobs, or operations as you normally define them in your current system may be required to complete each unit operation (a major transformation in the throughput).

APPLICATIONS

For the shirt laundering example, there are four identified state changes (each is a unit operation). Checking for wrinkles and spots is not a unit operation and neither is loading a washer. Unit operations are: (1) receive and tag, (2) wash and clean, (3) dry and press, (4) package and deliver.

that has been defined and approved. Worksheets are provided and explained for unit operation definition (see Figure 3-4). The entering and exiting throughput states are similar to the concept of beginning and ending inventory. The entering state of throughput for unit operation 1 is the demand for service; the exiting state from 1 is the entering state for 2 and so on; the final exiting state is the service system output. Information supplied on the right-hand side of the form is gathered only to reconcile differences in definition and description of unit operations.

Group B is split into pairs according to similar organizational level. Each pair is assigned the task of defining unit operations by completing the worksheets (each pair is given 10 to 15 worksheets). Each pair is required to work independently of all other pairs. It must be emphasized that pairs are not to communicate with each other. No examples for the current system are given nor are participants allowed to give one. Assistance can be sought from fellow employees provided that other employees do not assist more than one pair. After each pair has had about one day to develop unit operations, separate meetings are held with each pair by the project coordinators. These meetings take approximately one hour and involve a presentation of unit operations by each pair to the project coordinators.

Following the receipt of input from each of the pairs from group B, the project coordinators reconcile differences and similarities using the detailed information provided. An attempt should be made to minimize the number of unit operations. One common set of unit operations is developed; unit operation names are given; exiting states are described for each unit operation; and a handout documenting these unit operations and states is developed. An example handout for the shirt process is shown in Figure 3-5.

Session 3: Generation of Deviations

Convening group B on day 3, a two- to three-hour session is needed to generate deviations for the unit operations. This session is conducted primarily through a structured group process known as the nominal group technique, which was discussed in Chapter 2. Procedures

Figure 3-4

Unit Operations Worksheet

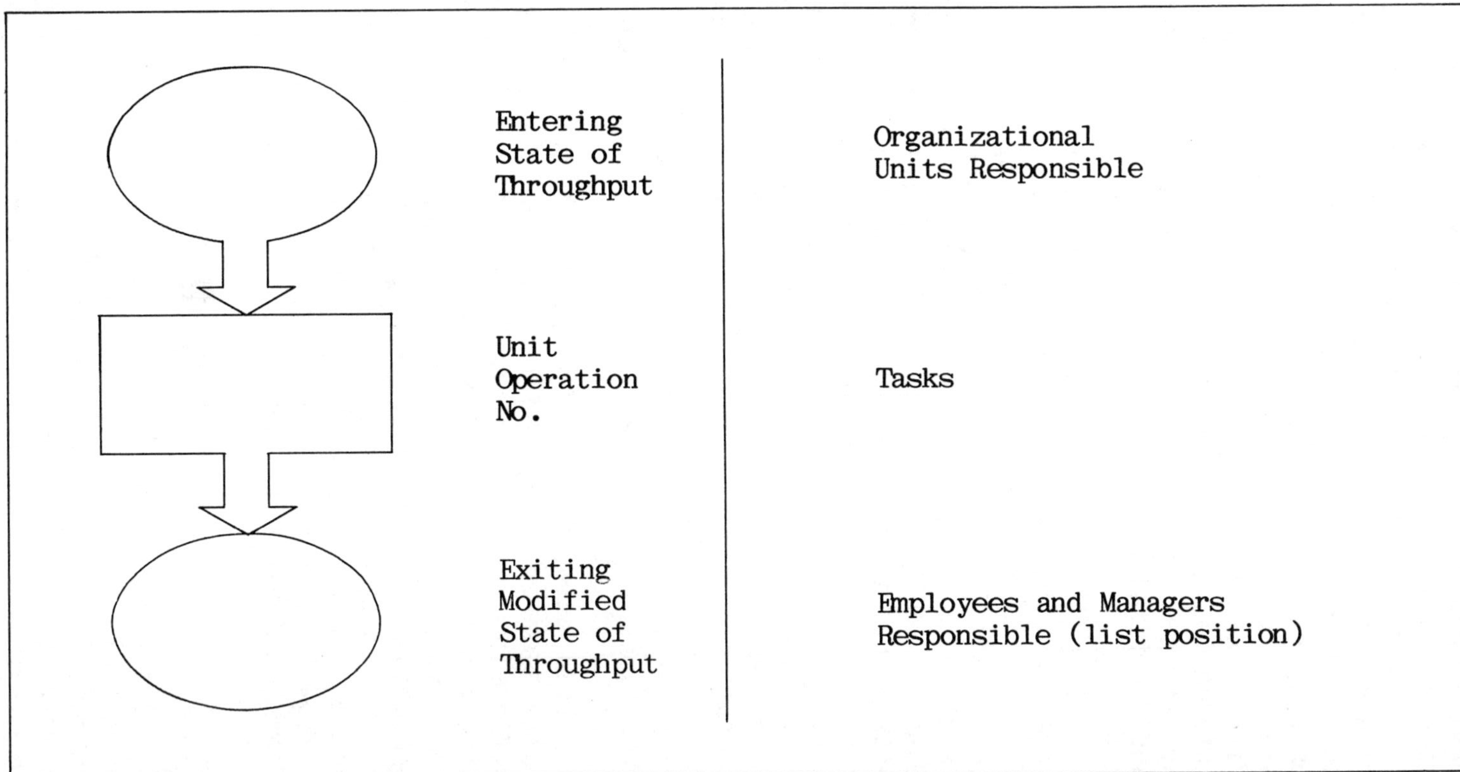

Figure 3-5

Handout on Unit Operations for Shirts

Demand: Soiled shirts presented by a customer

Unit Operations		Exiting State
U-1	Receive and tag	Identified and dated shirts
U-2	Wash and clean	Wet, unsoiled shirts
U-3	Dry and press	Shirts ready to wear
U-4	Package and deliver	Clean shirts presented to customer

will be described in detail here and then abbreviated for the measurement session, which also uses the nominal group method.

Prior to beginning the generation of deviations, the coordinators' synthesis of unit operations is presented and discussed. Any remaining differences must be reconciled at this time. The concept of deviations must be explained further also. Figure 3-6 presents a handout used to clarify the meaning and use of the term "deviation." Figure 3-7 is also a handout given participants that illustrates deviations for the shirt laundering example. It should be stressed that these are not all possible deviations for shirt laundering. Examples for the current system being analyzed are not allowed. The group process to be used is then briefly explained to the group. The basic steps are:

1. silent individual generation of deviations
2. round robin listing of deviations on flip charts
3. clarification of listed deviations
4. selection and voting on most important deviations
5. election and voting on most important <u>quality</u> deviations

Figure 3-6

Handout on Deviations

DEVIATION CHARACTERISTICS

1. Deviations represent technical system requirements that are subject to variability and that need to be controlled.

2. These deviations (variations) are caused by the nature of items submitted for service, the nature of unit operations, or the characteristics of throughput entering the leaving unit operations.

3. We are only concerned with those deviations for which a difference from the norm or standard has an impact on the ability of the system to meet target accomplishments for quantity, quality, cost, or other system objectives.

4. At this stage in the analysis we are concerned with what can be different in throughput, but not why.

    a. Faults in the current technical subsystems (such as a breakdown) and faults in the current social subsystems (such as maloperation of equipment) are not the focus.

    b. The focus is on throughput variations.

Figure 3-7

Handout on Deviations for Laundry Example

LAUNDERING SYSTEM DEVIATIONS

Description	Location Introduced*
1. Number, type, and size of stains in shirts	D, U-2
2. Number of buttons missing	D, U-2, U-3
3. Item identification missing	U-1, U-2, U-3
4. Wrong availability	U-4
5. Days until delivery	U-2, U-3, U-4

*Refers to the source of the deviation in terms of demand (D) or one of the unit operations (U-1, U-2, etc.) previously defined. Note that some deviations may be caused in several locations.

Silent Generation. Each member of group B is given a page with a question. Each participant has a copy of the system boundaries and unit operations. Participants are given ten minutes to write down deviations and the locations introduced for each; it is stressed that all should work hard for the full ten minutes. No comments or interruptions are allowed during this ten-minute period; participants are asked to do the best that they can with given information and definitions. The question posed for the shirt laundering example would be:

> What deviations (variations) do you believe have an impact in shirt laundering? After listing the deviation, please note beside the deviation the point in shirt laundering (D, U-1, U-2, U-3, U-4) where this deviation is introduced.

Participants are asked to consider the entire system, not just personal responsibilities.

Round Robin Listing. This session is essentially one of controlled group brainstorming. No discussion, reaction, clarification, or support is allowed as each person is asked to present a deviation. Only one deviation is presented by each person per round. It is extremely important that no reactions by the coordinators or other participants be allowed. One coordinator guides the round robin presentation by calling on each person in the same order each round. The other coordinator writes each deviation on flip charts in numbered sequence with the code for location introduced. The only allowed interaction is among the two coordinators and the participant when it is necessary to abbreviate the deviation offered. It is important that all deviations be posted in a location visible to all participants at all times. Each person is asked to pass or present a deviation during each round. A pass is for that round only and does not mean that the individual cannot offer a deviation in the next or any following round. Participants are not required to submit the worksheet used during the silent generation period. This is important so that group members do not feel a need to present what they have listed should they find that they had misinterpreted instructions or just listed some inappropriate items. It is very important to stress that deviations presented do not have to be on an individual's list; the group procedure may trigger additional or different ideas as it progresses. The purpose is to have a free flow of all ideas during this period; thus the importance of no reactions must be stressed and enforced. Participants are asked to listen to and look back at other deviations so that an "identical" deviation is not presented. Each person is also asked to indicate the sources (demand and/or unit operation number) of the deviation as it is presented. The round robin presentation continues without interruption and speedily until every person passes during the same round. When a pass round is finally achieved, the group is asked to examine the listing silently for two minutes to see if all unit operations have been adequately considered. The round robin presentation is then continued until another pass round is completed. Normally, 30 to 100 deviations are generated.

<u>Clarification</u>. Discussion regarding deviations is allowed during this time period; however, it is vital that two restrictions be explained and enforced. First, only clarification can be asked or given; individuals are not allowed to "sell" a deviation. Second, deviations are not identified by the person who offered them; the results are attributed only to the group, and any person can clarify any listed deviation. All participants and the coordinators may ask for clarification, offer clarification or rewording, suggest combinations of duplicate items, suggest elimination or break-up of deviations that are too general, suggest revisions in the source list for a deviation, or suggest the addition of a new deviation. It is efficient to examine one chart sheet at a time. It is necessary to continue the clarification period until all deviations are understood by all participants and coordinators. Normally, the clarification period will take about 30-45 minutes.

<u>Selection and Ranking</u>. Once the clarification period is ended, questions regarding deviations are not allowed, and individuals are asked to work silently and individually. First, each person is provided with eight blank cards. The lead coordinator then allows five minutes for each person to select the eight most important deviations and write the number and name of each of the eight on a separate card. Participants are not allowed to identify themselves on the cards. Again, it is useful for participants to examine and select from one chart at a time and then make a final selection from this smaller set. Importance is defined as "a deviation being critical as you perceive it with regard to accomplishment of perceived system goals and objectives."

When all participants have completed selection of exactly eight deviations and written one per card, they are asked to select the most important one of the eight and place an "8" with a circle around it in the upper right-hand corner of the card. Then they are asked to select the least important of the remaining seven and put a "1" in the upper right-hand corner of the card. Then participants are asked to finish ranking the remaining six important deviations with weights 7 through 2. When finished with this process, each participant should have the cards ordered from most to least important with weights of 8, 7, 6, 5, 4, 3, 2, and 1, respectively. This is a forced choice ranking; no ties are allowed to an individual. All cards are collected when the task is completed.

Quality Deviations. A second selection and ranking is conducted. Each person is given five blank cards. Quality is defined as "your own perception of quality for demand, throughput, and output of the defined system, remembering that timeliness is a part of the quality dimension." Each person is asked to select the five deviations most related to quality and to write the number and name of each on a separate card.

Selection is made from the complete list of deviations. Each person is then asked to do a forced choice ranking giving weights of 5, 4, 3, 2, and 1 from most to least important, respectively, for the five quality deviations selected. This second selection forces participants to consider the difference between quantity and quality. If measures are needed for both quantity and quality, this second selection is dropped.

KEY QUALITY DEVIATIONS

The information gained and documented from the sessions just described provides the foundation for a major phase of the process--the selection of the key quality deviations. Interestingly, the procedure that has been described thus far did not concern quality directly until the final selection and ranking of "quality deviations." The project coordinators are responsible for working jointly to establish the key quality deviations.

First, the voting is tabulated for key deviations and key quality deviations. The total point count and the number selecting each deviation are the relevant totals. The clearly preferred deviations resulting from the voting on quality deviations are listed first among the key quality deviations. These are clearly identified as key quality deviations when presented back to the groups. The number of these will normally range from a few more than the number of unit operations to twice the number of unit operations. At this point, the coordinator analyzes the remaining deviations that received some vote in the selection process. The coordinator then selects additional key quality deviations, taking into account the following factors:

1. frequency of occurrence
2. cost and time required to correct or deal with the deviation
3. impact of deviation on subsequent unit operations
4. impact of deviation on the customer
5. partial or similar coverage already by another key quality deviation (the possibility for combining exists)
6. selection of a deviation as the most important by at least one person
7. need for a key deviation related to each unit operation unless unusual circumstances exist for the unit operation's not being covered

Differences in voting results among important deviations and important quality deviations help to determine which deviations are or are not considered quality related.

If the coordinators are not comfortable with their level of familiarity with the function or organization being analyzed, it is recommended that a technical expert from the organization be asked to comment on the results obtained. This person should be someone with prior experience in the function who does not participate in any part of the rest of the process. A third-party facilitator can provide explanation of deviations, suggest omissions or needed combinations, and provide an additional selection and ranking of the key quality deviations. Thus, verification of the process results, and modifications needed to correct coordinators' biases can be made.

A set of key quality deviations is finalized and a handout listing them and the corresponding locations introduced is prepared. The quality deviations receiving the most votes should be listed first. Again, it is important that the coordinators be fair, knowledgeable in the function, and trained regarding the procedure for this portion of the process. The group session on generating measures should follow the other group sessions within a day or two; thus the project coordinators should act quickly in determining key quality deviations.

GROUP SESSIONS FOR MEASURES

Two sessions are required to gather input from system participants on creation of productivity measures and indicators for each deviation. The first session requires both groups A and B and is a nominal group session. The second involves group B only and is not structured.

Session 4: Generation of Measures

The structured group process that was used in the deviation generation session is used again. Only details that differ are discussed here; the nature of the process itself is not reviewed again. The purpose of this joint session of groups A and B is to generate possible measures related to outcomes and costs of the key quality deviations. About three hours are required to complete the session.

Explanation of Concepts. The terminology and process to be followed is explained and the meaning of deviations and key quality deviations is reviewed (especially for group A, which did not participate in the development of these). The steps in the process for this session are outlined as follows:

1. presentation of key quality deviations
2. 20 minutes for silent generation of measures for all key quality deviations
3. round robin listing of measures
4. clarification period for measures

There is no selection and voting phase as it would be inappropriate at this time. Evaluation of measures is done by group A at a later time.

The key quality deviations are presented and the nature of selection is explained. Participants are given a handout and are also requested to have the system boundaries and unit operations handouts with them. The few key quality deviations that received the most votes are identified and the criteria for selecting remaining deviations are disussed briefly. An opportunity to ask questions of clarification is provided. Although suggestions for additions are not solicited, if someone suggests adding a deviation, the group is asked to make the decision to include or exclude another deviation. The concept of measures, particularly productivity measures, must be thoroughly explained. The following discussion is to be provided by the lead project coordinator:

> Measures should deal with outcomes and resource use associated with a particular key quality deviation. Measures are needed for outputs, inputs, and output-input relationships. Output measures deal with the effect of the deviation on throughput and service output. Inputs deal with identifiable resources required to prevent the deviation or to deal with the result of the deviation. Some outcomes are directly associated with inputs used to attempt to avoid the outcome or to correct the outcome; such direct relationships can be measured by some ratio of output to input. Measures should deal with control, performance, actual versus standard, type of performance, degree of performance, count, cost impact, disruption impact, missed deadlines caused, both customer and internal impact, resources consumed in related social and technical subsystems for control, reduction, correction, prevention, percent of total effort on a particular deviation, and so on. What we want is a way to keep score for each of the key quality deviations.

Following this discussion, example measures are provided for the example deviations (Figure 3-7) given for the shirt laundering situation. The handout used is shown in Figure 3-8. These are discussed and a period of clarification questions by participants is allowed. Participants are not allowed to ask or give an example for the system being analyzed. Creative and open responses are sought; technical correctness of productivity ratios is achieved at a later stage.

Silent Generation. The next phase is to ask all participants to work for 20 minutes listing measures for each of the key quality deviations on a blank sheet provided. All participants are to work on all key

Figure 3-8

Handout on Measures for Laundry Example

MEASURES FOR FIVE EXAMPLE LAUNDRY DEVIATIONS

Deviation 1. Number, type, and size of shirt stains

Measure 1. Number of customer stain complaints / number of customers
2. Labor hours expended removing stains
3. Cost of shirt replacements / standard cost for replacements
4. Number of shirts with a stain / total number of shirts received

Deviation 2. Number of buttons missing

Measure 1. Number of shirts returned for replacement of buttons / number of shirts processed
2. Dollars of direct labor in button replacement / total direct labor dollars
3. Number of complaints of missing buttons / total cost to detect and correct missing buttons

Deviation 3. Item identification missing

Measure 1. Number of unidentified items / total item volume
2. Payments to customers for lost items / total revenue

Deviation 4. Wrong availability

Measure 1. Number of items returned / number of missing items reported
2. Total labor hours correcting wrong availability / total labor hours
3. Cost of shirt replacements for missing claims

Deviation 5. Days until delivery

Measure 1. Average time between receipt and delivery / standard processing time
2. Number of late deliveries / number of deliveries
3. Number of late shirt-days
4. Number of on-time deliveries / total delivery cost
5. Delivery cost per shirt

quality deviations during this time; again silence will be enforced. Participants are asked to list measures and their associated key quality deviations.

Round Robin Listing. A round robin listing procedure like that described for deviations is used to list all measures that the group has either listed during the silent generation period or can think of during the round robin listing. No restrictions are to be imposed about the order of dealing with deviations or type of measure; the round robin listing should be kept free flowing, and no more than one measure and 30 seconds should be allowed for each participant per round. Once a pass round is achieved, 2 minutes of silence is allowed for participants to look through lists posted and consider whether all key quality deviations have been adequately covered. Then the round robin listing is continued until another pass round is achieved.

Clarification Period. A clarification period for the measures is conducted under the same rules used during the clarification period for deviations. It is important that all group members and the project coordinators have a mutual understanding of all listed measures and that each measure listed has a definite relationship to one or more of the key quality deviations. The merits of measures cannot be discussed.

No selection or voting on the measures takes place during this session. Group A will be asked to complete a questionnaire evaluating refined measures for each deviation at a later stage.

TECHNOLOGY AND SYSTEM INPUT ANALYSIS

Session 5: Identification of Technical and Social Subsystems

Group B is convened for a two-hour meeting on the day following the measures session. The purpose of this session is to identify technical and social subsystems and actions related to the prevention and control of the key quality deviations. The procedure is less structured in that open discussion and interaction are allowed during responses to questions. Group B members are asked the same questions regarding each of the key deviations by one of the coordinators. Questions to be answered for each deviation cover where the deviation is dealt with and what resources are used. The questions are:

1. Which unit operations are involved in preventing, eliminating, and correcting the deviation and its organizational impact?
2. How is the deviation prevented, eliminated, reduced, and corrected with current personnel, systems, and procedures?
3. What technical subsystems have been recently installed or are planned that deal with or have an influence on the deviation?

Technical subsystems include such things as equipment, computer hardware, computer software and programming, computer operation time, purchased or developed special systems and aids, development of procedures, printed materials and manuals, and other one-time developments. The questions are asked in order for each deviation, and notes are taken by the coordinator during an open response and discussion period after each deviation. The coordinator probes and asks additional questions as needed to get complete information.

TRANSFORMATION OF RESULTS INTO PRODUCTIVITY RATIOS AND INDICATORS

Organization of Results

The results of the process to this point include (1) the unit operations, (2) the list of key quality deviations, (3) a list of possible measures, and (4) notes on locations and subsystems that deal with each key deviation. Prior to a final development of productivity measures, the results must be rearranged and summarized. The two coordinators carry out this phase. If coordinators do not have the expertise, this analysis can be done in conjunction with an analyst more familiar with productivity measurement.

Reorganization of Measures

The long list of measures created by the combined groups is in no particular order. One project coordinator rearranges measures by first listing all measures that may apply to each key quality deviation. Then, the coordinator analyzes the measures under a single deviation to combine duplicates and eliminate any that do not deal with outputs, inputs, or both. Also, any measures that do not relate to quality may be dropped. Factors listed that are an excuse for poor quality or plans for improving quality are eliminated. For the measures listed under each key deviation, subgroups of measures are formed related to particular quality characteristics. Finally, for each key deviation, a subgroup of all measures dealing with some input resource consumed is formed (particularly those dealing with dollar cost or labor hours).

Identification of Resources

The second coordinator analyzes the technical and social system notes from responses to the three questions of session 5 to identify resources consumed for each deviation or affected by a deviation. Resources include factors such as capital usage required, equipment, materials, labor hours, and manager hours. The factors and unit operations having particular impact have been identified by the questions and described in some detail. The coordinator must put the subsystem usage into possible input measure forms such as labor hours, expense per year, annual accounting charges for use, dollar investment, equivalent cost for capital usage, operating cost, labor hours required to conduct a special control procedure, and resource capacity lost by stoppage due to a deviation. The group session to generate measures usually provides mostly performance measures; the analysis and reduction of technical and social subsystem data provide more complete consideration of the input dimension of productivity.

Selection of Measures

The final selection and evaluation of productivity measures for each key quality deviation is a joint procedure for coordinators and participants. The two coordinators work together from the organized results for each key deviation to form a set or family of output-input productivity ratios. Because some measures do not fit into productivity ratios meaningfully, they must remain in a nonratio form and be considered productivity indicators. Once the sets of measures for key deviations are finalized, they are put in questionnaire form by the coordinators, and all members of group A are asked to evaluate the potential productivity measures individually (thus leading to selection and ranking).

Development of Ratios. The ratios are developed by the coordinators based upon their knowledge of the meaning and measurement of productivity. The ratios must be stated in a form that makes sense in terms of improvement. Typically, for ratios, it is necessary for the output numerator to be improved by increasing it and for the input denominator to be improved by decreasing it. Thus, the total productivity ratio itself reflects improvement by an increase in its value, regardless of the particular units or dimensions of the ratio. Numerators are generally stated as a percentage not having some unwanted quality characteristic, such as the "percentage of shirts not missing buttons." It is important to remember that any one productivity ratio has meaning only in relation to a complete set of measures for each deviation.

Productivity Indicators. The coordinators must not arbitrarily omit a measure or force an unmeaningful ratio. Items not subject to ratio statement are simply listed and are considered to be productivity indicators. The set of productivity measures and indicators is actually the result of the group session on measures; the coordinators have only changed the form where needed to create true productivity ratios. Only measures that were clearly duplicates, clearly not input and/or output, or clearly not quality may be eliminated by the coordinators. Also, several related measures may be combined into one productivity ratio.

Some measures may appear in similar form across most of the key deviations. If the measure can be stated in a similar fashion so that it is a summary measure for all related key deviations, then some system measures may be created for further evaluation.

CLARIFICATION OF EDITED MEASURES

Clarification Session

Since the list of edited measures includes a considerable amount of restatement and reorganization of measures and resources provided during the sessions, it has been found that a clarification session is needed before participants can rate the measures. The clarification period is begun by explaining the form of quality-productivity ratios (as was shown in equation 2-2). The list of measures is then distributed and informal questions and answers about each measure are allowed. All measures for a single deviation are covered before discussing the next deviation. Measures are listed under each deviation in order of being most like like a QPR. Clarification only is allowed; no evaluative comments are appropriate at this time. Measures may be rewritten or added by the group during the session. Coordinators may have to rewrite others following the session. An example QPR for the shirt laundry is:

$$\frac{\text{Number of shirts delivered by promised date}}{\left[\begin{array}{c}\text{Total}\\ \text{number}\\ \text{of shirts}\\ \text{processed}\end{array} \times \begin{array}{c}\text{process-}\\ \text{ing cost}\\ \text{per}\\ \text{shirt}\end{array}\right] + \left[\begin{array}{c}\text{number}\\ \text{of late}\\ \text{shirt}\\ \text{deliveries}\end{array} \times \begin{array}{c}\text{cost to expedite}\\ \text{late shirt deliv-}\\ \text{eries and answer}\\ \text{complaints}\end{array}\right]}$$

Clarification Participation

Participation in this session depends on the organization's implementation plans. If the organization is unsure about installing the measures or is planning only a partial installation of measures, then only group A is included in this session and the following session on ranking. This allows top management to screen the measures and select the most useful from a management perspective. If a complete installation of a quality measurement system is anticipated, the inclusion of group B in these two steps helps to provide a sense of ownership and understanding for all involved.

Evaluation of Measures

Questionnaire. Each member of group A is asked to complete a questionnaire to evaluate the sets of productivity measures. The instructions for the questionnaire with example questions for the shirt laundering system are given in Figure 3-9. A Likert-type rating procedure is utilized throughout. The measures for each deviation are listed in the same form for the rest of the questionnaire. The participants are asked to rate the measure in terms of its strength in measuring the value outcome of the deviation and then rate the strength of their belief in the first rating.

Figure 3-9

Productivity Measures Evaluation Questionnaire

GENERAL INSTRUCTIONS

Since meeting with you, we have reorganized the measures that your group suggested. We are now asking you to give us YOUR OPINION AS TO THE IMPORTANCE OF THE MEASURES PREVIOUSLY SUGGESTED. There are no right or wrong answers. We are interested in your opinion, that is, your feelings or beliefs. If you have no opinion on any measure leave the question blank.

When you have finished the questionnaire, place it in the brown envelope attached and seal it. Return the questionnaire to the person who gave it to you for collection and return to the project coordinators. No one except the project coordinators will see your response; the questionnaires will be summarized and then destroyed by the two coordinators.

MARKING THE QUESTIONNAIRE

For each deviation you will be asked to express your opinion about one or more measures relating to that deviation. You should check (1) the degree that you believe the measure relates to the deviation (from poor to good) and (2) your degree of certainty concerning your answser (from very strong to moderate).

Figure 3-9 (continued)

The following is an illustration from the activity laundering a shirt

<u>Deviation</u>: Buttons missing on shirts

<u>Measures</u>:

1. Buttons sewn on shirts / labor hours sewing buttons

   I believe this measure for this deviation is

   ○ Poor ○ Satisfactory ✓ Good

   I feel that my degree of certainty is

   ○ Very Strong ✓ Strong ○ Moderate

2. Shirts ironed / pounds of soap consumed

   I believe this measure for this deviation is

   ✓ Poor ○ Satisfactory ○ Good

   I feel that my degree of certainty is

   ✓ Very Strong ○ Strong ○ Moderate

The person who completed the above believed that the first measure, buttons sewn on shirt / labor hours in sewing buttons, was a good measure and felt strongly about this being so. Regarding the second measure, shirts ironed / pounds of soap consumed, the person believed this to be a poor measure for the deviation. Further, the person felt very strongly about this being a poor measure.

As you answer the questions in the balance of the questionnaire, remember that there are no right or wrong answers.

Scoring. For scoring the questionnaire results, the following scales are applied to each evaluation for each measure:

Response 1 (belief in measure)	Score
Poor	-0.8
Satisfactory	0.1
Good	1.0
Response 2 (degree of certainty)	
Very strong	0.9
Strong	0.5
Moderate	0.1

An individual score for a measure is a multiple of the scores for responses 1 and 2, respectively. The resulting measure score ranges from -0.72 up to +0.90. The scoring for the two responses was selected to reflect response 1 as being more critical than response 2.

Selection and Ranking. The group evaluation score for each measure is the average of the multiple scores across all respondents who chose to evaluate that measure. Only measures whose average is +0.05 or higher are selected by the research team for inclusion in the measurement system. This reflects at least a satisfactory belief in the measure with a strong degree of certainty. The measures selected are ordered from highest to lowest average for each deviation.

SELECTING THE FINAL QUALITY-PRODUCTIVITY MEASUREMENT SET

Overview

Top management, in conjunction with the operating supervisors, should make the final productivity measurement package selection. In most cases some measures will already exist; others will be judged valuable but too expensive to collect. At this stage it is critical that top management realize that substantially all of the measures development involved the work of their own employees. The coordinators mostly coordinated; the employees provided the expertise. The only exception was in the phase in which employee-generated measures were transformed into productivity measures or were left as indicators by the coordinators. In summary, the set of quality measures is organization generated and the organization should make the final productivity measurement selection and commitment. Without that commitment, it is doubtful that measurement would lead to improvement. For a true set of productivity ratios, the selected measures are further evaluated by the coordinators to produce ratios of two types. Quality-productivity ratios may be stated as either process or prevention ratios. A measurement "expert" may be needed to assist with this final task. The coordinators must serve as productivity measurement analysts during this last step. Guidance to coordinators is provided in the following definitions and examples.

Process Quality-Productivity Ratios

One of the two major types of quality-productivity ratios is a direct function of processing capabilities. The process quality-productivity ratio has the following general form:

$$QPR = \frac{A}{pU + cE} \qquad (3\text{-}1)$$

where:

- A = number of units acceptable and free of errors
- U = number of units processed
- E = number of units subjected to correction procedures
- p = processing cost per unit
- c = cost per unit for correction processing

In this form, the ratio dimensions are number of "good" units produced per dollar spent to produce and correct. Perhaps the reciprocal of the ratio provides a more readily recognized form: cost per unit. An example ratio for a personnel function is

$$QPR = \frac{\text{number of personnel files current and free of errors}}{\text{(Labor, equipment, and design cost per employee file)} \times \text{(number of employees)} + \text{(cost per correction)} \times \text{(number of corrections initiated)}}$$

Making this conceptual ratio practical for implementation requires defining terms and gathering both standard and special data. Definition of good items, files for the example, is the key to making a quality measure. This requires precise definition of significant errors, characteristics of "good" files, and standards for timeliness of information. Gathering data on the number of good files would most likely be done by a random sampling procedure rather than by a complete population census. The process cost per file would require inclusion of values that would be updated periodically according to accounting conventions. Costs would include allocation of costs for "overhead" factors such as design, equipment investment, and space. Primary variable costs, based upon current actual values, would include items such as labor cost, inspection cost, and computer charges computed per file.

Part of the cost of producing acceptable personnel files is reworking or correcting files that are out of date or erroneous. Actual level of quality is a function of both the normal process of handling personnel files and regular efforts to inspect and correct files. Both costs are included in the denominator of the process quality-productivity ratio.

Prevention Quality-Productivity Ratios

The second major class of quality-productivity ratios includes measures for systems to prevent inferior or unacceptable quality. A prevention quality-productivity ratio has the following general form:

$$QPR = \frac{S}{D + M + Z} \tag{3-2}$$

where:

- S = percentage of employees (or other appropriate bank unit) satisfactorily serviced annually
- D = development cost allocated yearly for this prevention system
- M = maintenance cost per year to execute the prevention system
- Z = special costs required by prevention system

Dimensions for the ratio are the percentage satisfactorily serviced per dollar spent to prevent unsatisfactory services. An example ratio for a personnel function is:

$$\text{QPR} = \frac{\text{Percentage of employees for whom no compensation complaints are filed}}{\begin{array}{c}\text{Annual cost allocation for salary structure design}\end{array} + \begin{array}{c}\text{(yearly compensation analysis cost per job category)} \times \text{(number of job categories)}\end{array} + \begin{array}{c}\text{(cost for handling a compensation inquiry)} \times \text{(number of compensation inquiries)}\end{array}}$$

Defining relevant costs and measuring the percentage serviced properly are special problems in making prevention quality-productivity measures operational. The numerator in the example would require cataloging both written and oral complaints registered with the personnel staff. If no formal procedure exists, then a survey instrument may have to be developed and administered to monitor perceived complaint levels.

In some instances, salary structures are created by special consultants, and thus the annual cost of that investment may be easy to identify. Otherwise, the combined efforts of several different groups may need to be given a value for measurement purposes. Additional development cost may also be required yearly. Annually, a special survey of regional and national compensation levels may be conducted prior to determination of salary ranges by job category. Specific labor survey and computer costs may be identified easily for maintenance costs. The cost to process salary inquiries and the effectiveness of handling such inquiries is a special cost.

Nature of Service Productivity Ratios

Productivity of services should be measured principally by quality-productivity ratios. The process quality-productivity ratio combines the user's concern for quality characteristics of services and an operational concern for costs to produce acceptable output units. Many of the functions of services are basically avoidance or prevention activities to maintain good employee, managerial, governmental, customer, or community relations. Prevention quality-productivity measures put these concerns into a form whereby the marginal benefits of added resource usage can be evaluated. Rather than enumerating activities carried out by service staff and comparing this list with currently recommended practices, the quality-productivity ratios allow yearly evaluations to concentrate on resources consumed to provide services that meet user quality standards. Using certain procedures does not assure meeting quality requirements for services; the impacts of activities and related costs are jointly included in the suggested ratio forms.

MEASUREMENT PROCEDURE SUMMARY

The basic steps in the methodology of creating a productivity measurement system for the quality dimension of a product or service function are summarized in Table 3-2. This table includes the activities of Table 3-1, estimated activity times, and estimated elapsed calendar time. The elapsed calendar time is not cumulative. Total calendar time to complete such a project would range from one to three months, depending upon resource commitments to the project. Included are a week of group sessions and about a week of measurement analysis and ranking that would be very difficult to reduce.

The result of this procedure is a family of productivity output-input measures for each key quality deviation. Also identified for each key quality deviation are the locations (unit operations or demand) of introduction and the locations (unit operations) at which the deviation must be handled. Thus a measurement system or package has been created for the quality dimension of the subject service function. The use of the measurement package depends on the original intent of the organization in conducting the project and technical, social, and economic feasibilities of implementing and operating the measurement package.

Table 3-2

Measurement Procedure Summary

Activity Sequence	Activity	Participants	Estimated Activity Time	Estimated Elapsed Calendar Time
1	Top management decision to measure productivity	Organization management	1/2 day	1–2 weeks
2	Select project coordinators	Organization management	1/2 day	1–2 weeks
3	Familiarize with system (function)	Project coordinators	1–2 days	1 week
4	Select participants; divide into groups	Project coordinators and top management	2–3 hours	2 days
5	Define system and establish boundaries	Project coordinators in consultation with top management	2 hours	1 day
6	Determine unit operations	Group B with project coordinators	4 hours	1 day
7	Generate deviations; select and rank deviations	Group B with coordinators	3 hours	1 day
8	Finalize key quality deviations	Project coordinators and possibly technical facilitator	2 hours	1 day

Table 3-2 (continued)

Activity Sequence	Activity	Participants	Estimated Activity Time	Estimated Elapsed Calendar Time
9	Generate key quality deviation measures	Groups A and B with coordinators	3 hours	1 day
10	Collect technology and system input data	Group B; individual experts with coordinators	2 hours	1 day
11	Edit measures into productivity ratios and indicators	Project coordinators or analyst	1 day	2 days
12	Clarify edited measures and revise as necessary	Group A with coordinators	3 hours	1 day
13	Put measures into questionnaire format	Project coordinators	1 day	1 week
14	Rank productivity measures by completing questionnaire	Group A with coordinators	2 hours	1 day
15	Evaluate questionnaire results and produce quality-productivity ratios	Project coordinators (and productivity ratio expert)	2–4 days	2–3 weeks

4
Results from the Federal Reserve Banks

This chapter presents detailed results of the measure development procedure that were obtained during a project sponsored by the National Science Foundation with the cooperation of three Federal Reserve bank districts. Whereas the previous chapter presented the measurement process through narrative and illustrations of forms used, this chapter depicts the process through data gathered by applying the process.

DESCRIPTION OF SITES

The Federal Reserve System

The Federal Reserve System has 12 relatively autonomous districts throughout the United States; some of the districts are subdivided into branch territories. In addition to the overall governing board for the system, each district has its own governing board to set policy and make major operations decisions. Although the districts have a high degree of autonomy, there is considerable communication and coordination among them.

Within the Federal Reserve System, three different districts were chosen; then one bank was selected from each district. Two of the three are district banks; the third is a large branch bank.

Organizational Functions

The research design indicated that the organizational functions to be studied should include both a quasi-manufacturing function and a nearly pure service. In bank A, a district bank, the check-processing function and the personnel function were studied. In bank B, the other district bank, the procedure was replicated only for the personnel function. In bank C, the branch bank, the procedure was replicated only for the check-processing function.

Check Processing

Check processing at the Federal Reserve bank is a quasi-manufacturing process in that a physical product is involved in the rendering of a service to the clients. Canceled checks arrive at the Federal Reserve where they are verified, sorted, and dispatched after appropriate debit and credit entries are made in the accounts of the member banks. Essentially, the process is one of transferring funds from the banks that have cashed the checks (drawer banks) to those upon whom the check was drawn (drawee banks).

Volumes differ considerably from one bank or district to another, but, in bank A, 120 employees process about one and a half million checks per day ($300 million) using high-speed reader/sorters and other peripheral equipment.

Two characteristics make the check-processing function different from most quasi-manufacturing processes. First, the product being processed is money; hence, there is an emphasis on accuracy and security. Second, the nature of the job requires that virtually all of the work that is received during a day be processed before the end of that working day. Strict deadlines are imposed for the submission of checks; however, any work left unprocessed must be held over, thereby incurring the opportunity cost of lost interest.

Personnel

Within guidelines set by the Federal Reserve System, each district bank carries out its own personnel activities similar to those in any large organization in the private or public sector. The function is typically organized under an officer who is responsible for wage and salary activities, benefits analysis and administration, recruiting and staffing, training and development, and record keeping. Generally, the district bank establishes policies, recruits professional staff, and completes reports for the district, while the branches administer policies and recruit technical and clerical personnel from the local area to carry out branch activities.

The number of employees, as well as the size and number of branches, differs from one district to the next. In bank A, 850 employees work at the district bank, while another 850 work in its three branches. Exclusive of payroll, the district bank has a personnel department staff of 14, and about 4 personnel specialists are employed by each branch. In bank B's district, 2,400 employees are divided among 775 at the district bank and 1,625 at the five branches. The personnel staff is slightly larger, with 17 persons in the district bank and about 5 in each branch.

RESEARCH RESULTS IN CHECK PROCESSING

Research results for check processing at bank C are presented for all steps except 12 and 15 (Table 3-1). Steps 12 and 15 had not been added to the procedure at the time we applied it at bank C. The results for check processing at bank A are not presented in this book (see Adam, Hershauer, and Ruch 1978 for complete results); results were similar but also unique to bank A. Bank C is presented because it was the second site and application of the process was more precise.

System Definition and Boundaries

The first step in the research procedure was to employ the aid of members of the organization to define and delimit the system to be studied. The result of that effort for bank C is shown in Figure 4-1.

Figure 4-1

System Boundaries for Check Processing (bank C)

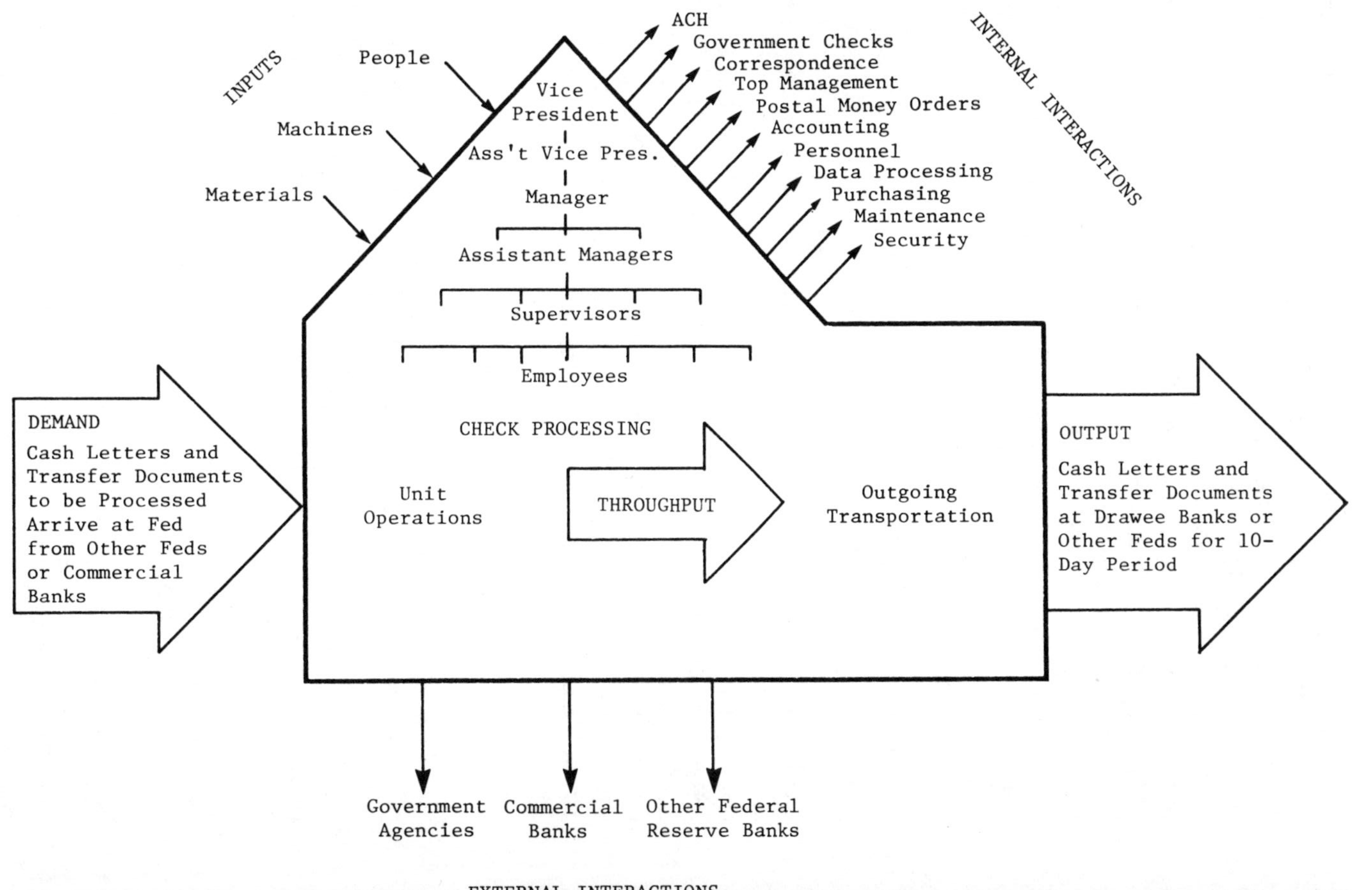

The system begins at the time and place that incoming cash letters and transfer documents arrive at the mailroom of the Federal Reserve bank; this constitutes a documentation of a request for transfer of funds. The system ends at the time and place that outgoing cash letters and transfer documents arrive at the drawee banks or another Federal Reserve bank or branch; this constitutes documentation that funds have been transferred. Note that, because of legal liabilities, outgoing transportation is a part of the system but incoming transportation is excluded. Inputs to the system are listed only by general categories.

The vice president of operations and those people and functions for which he or she is responsible are within the system. Relationships among these people are internal to the system. An internal interaction is a relationship of some part of this system with another system within the bank. For example, the relationship of the vice president (part of "top management") is an internal interaction. The most common internal interactions are noted.

External interactions are direct relationships of this system with organizational units outside of this Federal Reserve bank. The major external interactions are specified.

The only major difference in system boundaries for the two banks studied was the placement of the automated clearinghouse outside systems boundaries at bank C.

This difference emphasizes the need for developing a systems boundary as an integral part of the research. Even if organizational units appear very similar, differences could exist that would prove critical in later stages of the research. Also, it is important to note that organizations change over time. Systems boundaries should be set or updated at the time that the remainder of the research is to be done.

Unit Operations

The second step in the research process is to determine unit operations by the procedure described in Chapter 3. Comparatively little disagreement was found among the participants, although each had slightly different viewpoints and terminology.

At bank C, an abbreviated procedure was followed. Participants were presented with the unit operations from the first site and were asked to verify or modify them to fit their organization. No significant changes were made except for that part dealing with the automated clearinghouse. The unit operations, as refined at the second site, are shown in Table 4-1.

Table 4-1

Unit Operations for Check Processing, Bank C

Unit Operations	Exiting State	Notes
U-1 Receipt of transfer documents	Documents time verified and made ready for preparation	"Transfer documents" includes (1) checks, (2) cash letters, (3) clearinghouse settlements, (4) direct-sent cash letters, (5) "fine-sort" cash letters and documents, (6) CD deposits from government agencies; includes time and content verification, segregation, traying, and/or documentation as required
U-2 Preparation for processing	Documents prepared for processing and credit encoding added	Includes control documentation and recap

Table 4-1 (continued)

Unit Operations	Exiting State	Notes
U-3 Processing	Credit and debit messages transferred, checks endpoint sorted, outgoing documents generated	Includes high-speed and low-speed processing
U-4 Reconciling and settlement	Transfer documents proved and correction notification sent to accounting	
U-5 Preparation for dispatch	Outgoing documents gathered, verified, packaged, and labeled for dispatch to endpoints	
U-6 Dispatch	Transfer documents received at desitination	Transportation performed by a variety of couriers but federal is responsible until delivered; destination may be commercial bank or other federal
U-7 Post-processing	Transfer documents accepted by drawee banks and transfer of funds completed	Includes returns by midnight of day following delivery; includes adjustments initiated within two weeks

Key Quality Deviations

Following the procedure described in Chapter 3, participants at bank C generated the deviations listed in Supplement A. From this list, seven key quality deviations were obtained. These are listed in Table 4-2 along with the notation for the unit operation at which they are introduced.

The key quality deviations at bank A included three deviations not included in the list at bank C. Bank A listed loss of audit trail, missorts, and loss of data as major deviations to be considered. Later discussions with executives from bank C revealed that these problems had been essentially eliminated by the installation of sophisticated sorting and tabulating equipment that had not yet been implemented in bank A. They conjectured that the two lists of key quality deviations would have been more similar had the equipment (level of technology) at the two banks been identical.

Table 4-2

Key Quality Deviations for Check Processing, Bank C

Deviation Reference Number	Deviation	Point at Which Deviation is Introduced
1	Work left to balance after dispatch	D, U-1, 2-4
2	Timeliness of dispatch	D, U-3, 5
3	Rejects and misread items	D, U-3
4	Inadequate information on entries	U-4
5	Credit or debit to wrong bank	U-2, 4
6	Misfiled, mislabeled, and missent cash letters	U-3, 5, 6
7	Holdover	D, U-1, 2

Measures for Key Quality Deviations

The next step in the research procedure was to develop measures for the key quality deviations. Only the measures generated in bank C are given (Supplement B), as the lists are lengthy and there is considerable overlap in the lists from the two sites.

Key quality deviations were used to generate measures. Column 1 of Supplement B lists one or more key quality deviations to which each measure applies. Some of the measures are in ratio format, while most are unitary measures. No effort is made during the generation of these measures to refine, combine, or eliminate items; refinement constitutes the next step in the procedure.

Refinement of the Ratios into Productivity Measures

Supplement C presents the information gathered on technology and system inputs. The questions that were used are also shown.

The information from Supplements B and C is then used by the project coordinators to develop the set of quality-productivity ratios and indicators. An attempt has been made to combine related performance and input factors wherever possible. However, similarity to original measures has been maintained so that participants will understand and recognize measures. In future applications, we have taken more liberty in molding measures, and therefore the procedure has been embellished by adding a clarification session after measure formation by the coordinators. The final set of measures developed for check processing at bank C is given in Supplement D.

The measures were put into questionnaire format as shown in Figure 3-9. Responses from the participants at bank C were obtained and scored according to the procedure described in Chapter 3. Average scores for each measure are also reported in Supplement D; accepted measures are marked with an asterisk (*). There are 35 measures shown, with a maximum of 8 and a minimum of 2 for a single deviation. The number accepted per deviation ranges from 1 to 5. The total number of accepted measures is 25. The participants' acceptance of measures as reflected in the responses to the measure evaluation questionnaire is a strong plus for the reasonableness of the approach. Similar acceptance rates have been experienced in all applications of the process.

RESEARCH RESULTS IN PERSONNEL

The research procedure used in the personnel functions at the two sites and the results derived parallel those in check processing. The results are presented, therefore, with little additional comment, as most of the descriptions of the check processing results also apply to personnel. The only significant differences are that all 15 steps were applied. Therefore, results are also available for step 12--clarification of measures--and step 15--final quality-productivity ratios developed by us.

Figure 4-2 portrays the systems boundaries for the personnel functions at both banks A and B. One diagram is sufficient, as there were no material differences between the two sites. Table 4-3 contains the unit operations for bank B, which, again, apply to both organizations. It should be noted that the lack of a physical product being transformed carries special problems in the analysis of the personnel function. For example, there was substantial agreement on the listing of the unit operations, but their sequence is somewhat arbitrary since a product flow does not form a basis for the serial performance of the operations.

The refined list of key quality deviations for bank A are listed in Table 4-4. Only results for bank A are given here (see Adam, Hershauer, and Ruch 1978 for complete details). Measures generated and the data on technical systems are omitted.

Measures were refined by the coordinators and then clarified by participants after the questionnaire had been administered. We added the clarification session after there was some confusion in understanding the refined measures. The clarification session is now a

Figure 4-2

Systems Boundaries for Personnel Function (bank B)

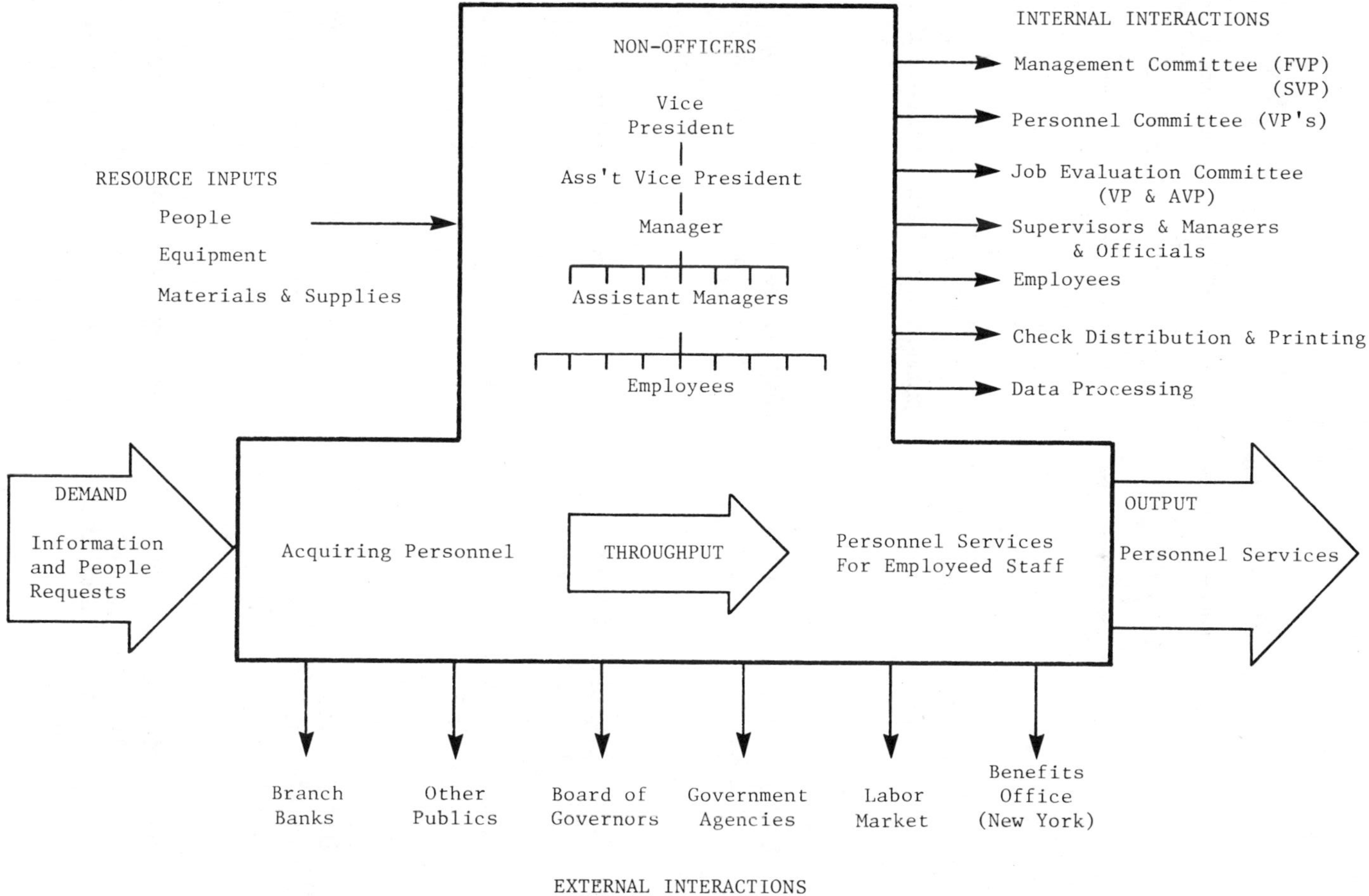

Table 4-3

Unit Operations for Personnel Function, Bank B

	Unit Operations	Exiting State
U-1	Recruit and employ staff	Employee starting work and personnel files established
U-2	Evaluate employee job assignments	Employees assigned to approved jobs and grade levels
U-3	Compensate employees: review and adjustment for wages, salaries, and benefits	Employees compensated in relation to market and performance
U-4	Train	Employee skills and career development enhanced
U-5	Administer personnel services to employees and the public	Employees retained, public information requests answered, and environment and morale enhanced by problem solving

Table 4-4

Key Quality Deviations for Personnel, Bank C

Deviation Reference Number	Deviation	Point at Which Deviation is Introduced
1	Misinterpretation by employees or personnel staff of bank policies and benefits	U-1, 5, 4
2	Employees inappropriately compensated	U-2, 3
3	Poor interpersonal communications with employee and/or applicant	U-1, 5
4	Lack of qualified applicants to staff departments (including EEOC considerations)	D, U-1
5	Salaries not in line with market	U-3
6	Incorrect benefits claim processing	D, U-5
7	Employee skill mismatched to job	U-1, 2
8	Mismatch of training and training needs	U-4
9	Deficient promotion assistance to department manager and to employee	U-5
10	Incorrect data: salary/benefit survey	U-3
11	Incorrect data: enrollment salary, grade, and benefits	U-1, 5

part of the measure development process. Since you have seen the complete data for check processing, data will not be presented for personnel. Instead, Tables 4-5 and 4-6 present refined measures for deviation 1 only, before and after clarification, respectively.

Many of the measures that have been presented in this chapter do not look like the process and prevention quality-productivity ratios presented in Chapter 3. We have found that the project coordinators, who are familiar with the output-to-input form, must take the group results and conduct further analysis to finally produce such measures. This analysis stage is now listed as step 15 in the process. Your own staff members can learn to conduct this analysis. One page of these results for personnel appeared in Table 3-2. An example set of final measures for one area of performance are presented in Table 4-7. These represent productivity measures ready for implementation.

SUMMARY

The primary purpose in presenting these data is to illustrate the prototypical procedure to develop measurement ratios for the quality dimension of productivity. The major conclusion is that the procedure works; in dissimilar organizational functions, the procedure yielded a number of acceptable measurement ratios capable of monitoring quality performance.

It is clear, however, that the measurement ratios derived in this application are unique both to the function within the firm and to the technology of the industry. Some similarities could exist between the measures of the personnel function in a Federal Reserve bank and the personnel function in, say, a steel manufacturing plant; but it would be impossible to apply exactly the same measures to both.

The procedure employed to develop the measures is sufficiently independent of the situation to be applied across a wide variety of functions and technologies involving products or services. No evidence exists at this time that indicates limits to the applicability of the procedure.

Table 4-5

Productivity Ratios and Indicators for Personnel: Generated, Scored, and Accepted, Bank A

Numerator	Denominator	Average Score
Deviation 1: Misinterpretation by employees or personnel staff of bank policies--benefits		
1.1 Percentage of employees not initiating questions or complaints concerning misinterpretations	Personnel costs	-.03
1.2 Percentage of employees not initiating questions or complaints	Manager labor hours + analyst labor hours + senior records clerk labor hours	.10†
1.3 Percentage of employees not filing grievance claims	Personnel costs	-.07
1.4 Percentage of employees not requiring exceptions to bank policies	Manager labor hours + analyst labor hours + senior records clerk labor hours	-.11
1.5 Percentage of employees in exit interview not mentioning bank policy misinterpretation	Personnel costs	.03
1.6 Percentage of employees in exit interview not mentioning bank policy misinterpretation	Annual costs for policy and benefits training program	.03
1.7 Number of lawsuits filed		-.15

†Accepted; score greater than +.050.

Table 4-6

Productivity Ratios and Indicators for Personnel: Generated, Scored, and Accepted, Bank A after Clarification

Numerator	Denominator	Average Score
Deviation 1: Misinterpretation by employees or personnel staff of bank policies--benefits		
1.1 Percentage of employees not initiating questions or complaints concerning misinterpretations	Personnel department costs	-.10
1.2 Percentage of employees not initiating questions or complaints	Total personnel staff labor hours	.11†
1.3 Percentage of employees not filing grievance claims	Personnel depart- costs	-.12
1.4 Percentage of employees not requiring exceptions to bank policies	Total personnel staff labor hours	-.03
1.5 Percentage of employees in exit interview not mentioning bank policy misinterpretation	Personnel department costs	-.98
1.6 Percentage of employees in exit interview not mentioning bank policy misinterpretation	Orientation and enrollment labor hours	.12†
1.7 Employee attitude index regarding misinterpretation of bank policies from a survey	Attitude survey costs + personnel department costs	.20†

†Accepted; score greater than +.050.

Table 4-7

Measures for Employee Interactions

Numerator	Denominator
1. Number of employees retained	(Number of employees continuing and hired) x (average personnel cost per employee) (includes costs for all personnel services plus surplus of employee compensation over equivalent market compensation)
2. Number of employees satisfied with interpersonal communications with the personnel department	(Number of employees) x (cost of personnel counseling and survey time per employee)
3. Percentage of correct employee responses on an organizational policy interpretation questionnaire	(Annual charges for orientation program development) + (orientation program and policy communication costs) + (cost of policy questionnaire administration including employee time lost)
4. Percentage of employees who feel that job descriptions are accurate and up to date	(Number of jobs analyzed) x (cost per job to analyze job requirements) + (number of job descriptions written) x (cost per job to prepare job descriptions)

Supplement A

All Deviations for Check Processing, Bank C

Deviation	Point at Which Deviation is Introduced
1. Missent bundles and cash letters	U-5, 6
2. Cash letter without items	D
3. Cash letter without info	D
4. Cash letter missing or delayed	D
5. Incomplete detail listing	U-5
6. Last-hour deposit in excess of capacity	D
7. Format variations in cash letter	D
8. Incorrect amount charged to drawee bank	U-3, 4
9. Entries written to wrong bank	U-4
10. Missent return items	U-3
11. (Voided)	
12. Cash letter with bundle missing	D, U-1, 2
13. Processing of wrong incoming cash letter	U-1, 2
14. (Voided)	
15. Late dispatch	D, U-3, 5
16. Improper identification of sending bank	U-2
17. Missing endorsements	D
18. (Voided)	
19. Entries charged to wrong bank	U-4
20. Extra bundles with cash letter	D
21. Items received without detail list	D
22. Malfunction of machine	U-3
23. Inadequate information on entries	U-4
24. Rejects and misread items	D, U-3
25. (Voided)	
26. Drawee bank returning own items	D
27. Errors found too late to adjust	U-4
28. Entries for unlocated differences	U-4
29. Bundle recaps missing	D
30. Items received without encoding	D
31. Items processed more than once	D, U-1, 2
32. Status of exception items not current	U-4
33. Correcting and updating automated credit and debit	U-4
34. Lack of reconciliation by sending bank	D

Supplement A (continued)

Deviation	Point at Which Deviation is Introduced
35. Cash letter delivered to wrong endpoint	U-6
36. Counterbalances in work	U-4
37. Lost cash letter	U-1, 2-6
38. Work run out of order	U-3, 4
39. Incorrect or missing federal endorsement	U-3
40. Time verification for credit of cash letter	U-1
41. Low-speed work processed on high-speed equipment	U-3
42. Work dropped	U-1, 3
43. Lost CLDs (direct-sent cash letter)	D, U-1
44. Wrong block numbers entered	U-3
45. Improper packaging incoming	D
46. No availability date on CLD	D
47. Proper placement of jam items	U-3
48. Work left to balance after dispatch	D, U-1, 2-4
49. Improper sorting of incoming work	U-1
50. Wrong corrections made on cash letter	U-3
51. Items mutilated	D, U-1, 2-6
52. Improper nine-digit number for credit of CLDs	D
53. Wrong sort program initiated	U-3
54. Work dispatched without cash letter or details	U-6
55. Holdover, high speed	D, U-1, 2
56. Correspondent bank relationship on fine sort not indicated	U-2
57. Improper fine-sort deposits	D
58. Grabby couriers	U-6
59. Many errors in reject listing	U-4
60. Missent direct-sent cash letter	D, U-1
61. Listed, not pocketed, items	U-4
62. Banding of two banks' work	U-5
63. Counterbalancing debit and credit written	U-4

Supplement A (continued)

Deviation	Point at Which Deviation is Introduced
64. Wrong bank credited	U-2, 3
65. Pocketed, not listed, items (piggyback)	U-4
66. Loose items	U-1, 2-5
67. Bundles too large to process on low speed (over 250 items)	U-4
68. Free item next to batch ticket	U-4
69. Requests for nonstandard information from drawee banks	D
70. Lack of clerk identification	U-4, 5, 6
71. Requests from drawee bank for cash letter totals	U-5, 6
72. Items unrelated to cash letter and tapes	D
73. Control documents misencoded	U-2
74. Cash letter dispatched with wrong total	U-5
75. Sorter throughput	U-3, 4
76. Dispatched mislabeled	U-3, 5
77. Work not dispatched	U-6
78. (Voided)	
79. Timely notification of changes in bank's correspondence or delivery	D
80. Items improperly placed by balancers	U-4
81. Exceptions to rules (sensitive banks)	D, U-1, 6
82. Notification of large amount adjustments	U-4
83. Incorrect correspondent bank on entry	U-4
84. (Voided)	
85. Photo items	D
86. Noncash items	D, U-1
87. Items in carriers	D
88. Items received loose from post office	D
89. Late-return items	U-7
90. "As of" reserve allowances	D, U-1, 4, 6, 7
91. Fine-sort cash letter not credited or charged	U-1
92. Items set up incorrectly	U-2
93. Work broken down incorrectly	U-2

Supplement B

Measures for Key Quality Deviations in Check Processing, Bank C

Key Quality Deviation Reference No.		Measure Description
1	1.	Work left / work processed
4, 6	2.	Number of cases times average time to resolve
4	3.	Volume of entries requiring verification / total entries prepared
7	4.	Total volume processed / total volume received
1	5.	Items left to balance / entries written on those items
3	6.	Number of rejects and misreads / total items processed
6	7.	Dollar amount missent / total dollar cash letters
3	8.	Dollar amount rejects / dollar amount processed
5	9.	Number of adjustments / number of credits or debits passed
2	10.	Frequency of late dispatch
1	11.	Number of errors reported in work dispatched unbalanced / number of errors reported in work dispatched unbalanced
6	12.	Number of missent cash letters / total number of cash letters dispatched
3	13.	Number of items killed for low-speed items run on high speed / number of rejects for low-speed run on high speed
1	14.	Actual number of blocks balanced / projected number of blocks that could be balanced by individual / actual number of blocks balanced

Supplement B (continued)

Key Quality Deviation Reference No.	Measure Description
1, 2, 4, 7	15. Total overtime (hours and dollars)
2	16. Cost of special runs / cost for courier service
7	17. Dollar holdover / dollars processed
5	18. Number of posting errors / number of posting transactions
1-3	19. Percentage machine downtime during critical time needed
6	20. Number of missent cash letters / number of cash letters mislabeled
3	21. Number of entries required to correct misreads during processing
7	22. Dollar holdover / dollars received
3	23. Rejects by pass for low speed on high speed / total number of items by pass
6	24. Number of hours spent advising of delay in presentation to drawee bank / number of items missent
6	25. Cost of correcting / cost of dispatch
1	26. Total item passes balanced / total item passed unbalanced
1	27. Frequency of entries written on certain banks
6	28. Number of missent cash letters / number of incorrect deliveries by couriers
4	29. Number of errors on adjustment entries
2	30. Number of endpoints delivered late (weighted by lateness) / number of endpoints

Supplement B (continued)

Key Quality Deviation Reference No.		Measure Description
5	31.	Cost of reversing or correcting errors / total cost of accounting
1	32.	Outgoing errors per 100,000 items processed
2	33.	Number of cash letter charges backed off (creates remittance float)
5	34.	Number of corrections on credit transfer / number of errors not corrected
1	35.	Number of blocks left to balance / number of personnel available
4	36.	Cost of correcting errors on adjustment entries
2	37.	Total volume of days with late dispatch / total volume
2	38.	Total dollars for special courier runs
1	39.	Volume to be balanced identified by pass / total volume processed
3	40.	Misread items / total items processed
1, 3	41.	Number of listing errors / lost time caused
5, 6	42.	Number of cases requiring reserve allowances (and dollar amount)
6	43.	Number of missent bundles / number of bundles dispatched
2	44.	Remittance float dollars
6	45.	Number of missent cash letters minus courier errors / number of cash letters dispatched
1, 2-3, 6-7	46a.	Cost per 1,000 items for checks
1, 2-3, 6-7	46b.	Cost per 1,000 cases for adjustments

Supplement B (continued)

Key Quality Deviation Reference No.		Measure Description
6	47.	Number of missent items / number of items dispatched
1, 2–3, 6–7	48.	Items / labor hours
2	49.	Labor hours on phone by auto charge clerk on late dispatch days / labor hours on phone by auto charge clerk on regular days
1–7	50.	Number of employees, absent, vacation, leave / total number of employees
1, 2, 7	51.	Percentage of last hours volume by depositor / total volume by depositor
7	52.	Cost to eliminate holdover
7	53.	Cost of culling large items
3	54.	Number of hours to balance low-speed run on high speed / number of hours to balance same volume of high speed on high speed
3	55.	Number of hours to manually process low speed / number of hours to process same volume on high speed
1, 2, 4–7	56.	Number of experienced personnel / number of inexperienced
3	57.	Percentage of jams and rejects / sorter operator
1	58.	Number of hours in restarts handled improperly by sorter operator
2	59.	Item pass ratio
1, 4–6	60.	Number of items correspondence / 100,000 items processed

Supplement C

Questions on Technical System Related to Impact on Deviations, Bank C

For each deviation the following two questions were asked of three members of group B:

1. Where is the deviation reduced, corrected, or eliminated?
   a. Which unit operation?
   b. How?
2. What technical subsystems are used to control the deviation in each of the unit operations identified in question 1?
   a. Description
   b. Investment costs and justification
   c. Operating costs

Note: Technical subsystems include such things as facilities, equipment, computers, software, material, manual or mechanical procedures, and worker-machine interface systems.

Deviation 1: Work left to balance after dispatch (D, U-1, 2-4)

1. U-4 Reconciling (manual).
2. High-volume nights cause greater deviation.
   New system is coming in June called DOS CHECKS that will allow fourth sorter and improve ability to handle high-volume nights.
   Image matching for all passes will be introduced in June. Only first pass image matching is done now.
   Image matching will help to identify problems with incoming items for particular banks.

Deviation 2: Timeliness of dispatch (D, U-3, 5)

1. U-6
   D by having city banks break up incoming work. Tough to get country banks and out-of-zone items to do this. As commercial banks get 3890s, they send higher volume because they can meet deadlines.

Supplement C (continued)

---

2. DOS CHECKS and fourth 3890 will "eliminate" timeliness problems caused by U-3 capacity.
   Get partial kill listings from FED CHECKS software now; will get complete listing by sorter with new system.
   Currently make many special dispatches.
   Transportation cost handled in another area; there is a budget.
   General services takes bids for transportation and then considers both bid and timing requirements.

Deviation 3: Rejects and misread items (D, U-3)

1. U-4 Would be corrected before dispatched.
   U-3 Operator would catch items by fanning.
   U-2 Breakdown of items not major.
2. Special software exists on 3890s so that when 25 consecutive items are rejected it automatically stops.
   Burroughs cannot read some items that 3890 will read (probably about 66 percent reduction in rejects).
   Software is handled by systems and program staff.

Deviation 4: Inadequate information on entries (U-4)

1. U-7 Adjustment necessary.
   U-4 If recurring problem.
2. Each bank requires different information.
   Clerk only knows what is needed if on incoming detailed sheets (kill listings).
   Standard procedures exist for writing entries.
   Banks often want you to do their work in tracing; Feds try, by policy, not to do this.

Deviation 5: Credit or debit to wrong bank (U-2, 4)

1. U-4 Introduced in U-2 or wrong nine-digit number in U-4.
   U-7 Ones introduced in U-4.

---

2. If data processor puts correspondent bank number on entries, this error could be eliminated.
   For auto credits and debits there is no chance of errors in computer system, but there could be errors when entered if that bank goes through correspondent bank.
   Since FED CHECKS in September 1976, erroneous entries are caused by missing incoming cash letters or not getting into auto credit and debit (these could be large dollar amounts).
   If each bank (mostly nonmember) used only one correspondent bank, this problem would be reduced. Policy is probably coming out in this area in near future.

Deviation 6: Misfiled, mislabeled, and missent cash letters (U-3, 5, 6)

1. U-5
   U-4 Random possibility if doing settlement and notice.
   U-7 For all missents.
   U-4 If misfiled or mislabeled, then could correct even if sent.
2. Sorter operator checks first bundle of each box.
   In dispatch, clerks should check label with items before starting details.
   Ten percent or more of errors are a result of courier (about five different couriers).
   Courier systems have set up sort patterns to help reduce missent cash letters; this doesn't really cause additional work here.

Deviation 7: Holdover (D, U-1, 2, 3)

1. U-2 and U-3 are real sources of problem. D could be if banks decided to bring all items in at midnight.
2. New 3890 sorter has pretty much eliminated this deviation because of faster throughput.

Supplement D

Productivity Ratios and Indicators for Check Processing: Generated, Scored, and Accepted, Bank C

Numerator	Denominator	Average Score
Deviation 1: Work left to balance after dispatch		
1.1 Percentage of items balanced before dispatch	Total labor hours in check processing	−.072
1.2 Percentage of prime runs balanced before dispatch	Labor hours in reconciling and settlement	.408†
1.3 Percentage of items left to balance after dispatch not caused by machine downtime	Actual processing cost per 1,000	−.125
1.4 Percentage of outgoing cash letters not causing correspondence about work left to balance	Dollar expense in reconciling and settlement + dollar expense in balancing and adjusting after dispatch	−.438
1.5 Actual number of blocks balance per labor hour	Standard number of blocks balance per labor hour	.692†
1.6 Total overtime dollars caused by work left to balance after dispatch	Total dollar expense in check processing	.050†
1.7 Percentage of items received that are left to balance after dispatch	Percentage of items received during last hour	.633†

†Accepted; score greater than +.050.

Supplement D (continued)

Numerator	Denominator	Average Score
Deviation 2: Timeliness of dispatch		
2.1 Percentage of cash letters dispatched on time	Labor hours in preparation for dispatch	-.043
2.2 Percentage of cash letters dispatched on time	Cost per 1,000	-.140
2.3 Dollar volume of cash letter charges backed off	Total cost of special courier runs + budgeted cost of courier service + cost of preparation for dispatch	.293†
2.4 Total cost of special courier runs	Total cost of special courier runs + budgeted cost of courier service + cost of preparation for dispatch	.125†
2.5 Total overtime dollars caused by late dispatch	Total dollar expense in check processing	-.063
2.6 Average daily volume on days with late dispatch	Average daily volume	.685†
2.7 Percentage of cash letters delivered late (categorized by degree of lateness)		.200†
2.8 Percentage of items received that are dispatched late	Percentage of items received during last hour	.833†

Supplement D (continued)

Numerator	Denominator	Average Score
Deviation 3: Rejects and misread items		
3.1 Percentage of items not rejected or misread	Dollar expense in processing (U-3) + dollar expense in reconciling and settlement	.215†
3.2 Percentage of high-speed items run on high speed that are not rejected or misread	Dollar expense in processing (U-3)	.567†
3.3 Percentage of low-speed items run on high speed that are not rejected or misread	Dollar expense in processing (U-3)	.900†
3.4 Number of listing errors	Total number of rejects processed	.543†
Deviation 4: Inadequate information on entries (introduced in Reconciling and Settlement)		
4.1 Percentage of entries prepared with adequate information	Labor hours in reconciling and settlement	.130†
4.2 Percentage of incoming kill listings not causing correspondence concerning inadequate information on entries	Cost of correcting inadequate information on entries + cost of reconciling and settlement	-.078

Supplement D (continued)

Numerator	Denominator	Average Score
Deviation 5: Credit or debit to wrong bank		
5.1 Percentage of credits or debits made correctly	Labor hours in preparation for processing + labor hours in reconciling and settlement	-.132
5.2 Percentage of outgoing cash letters not causing correspondence about credit or debit to wrong bank	Dollar expense in preparation for processing + dollar expense in reconciliation and settlement + dollar expense in adjusting credits or debits to wrong bank	.160†
5.3 Percentage of credits or debits to wrong bank that do not require a postprocessing adjustment	Dollar expense in reconciliation and settlement + dollar expense in adjusting credits or debits to wrong bank	.068†
5.4 Dollar amount of adjustments for credit or debit to wrong bank	Total dollars processed	.083†
5.5 Dollar expense in adjusting credits or debits to wrong bank	Dollar expense of the adjustment function	.213†

Supplement D (continued)

Numerator	Denominator	Average Score
Deviation 6: Misfiled, mislabeled, and missent cash letters (introduced in Processing, Preparation for Dispatch, and Dispatch)		
6.1 Percentage of outgoing cash letters not misfiled, mislabeled, or missent by noncourier error	Labor hours in preparation for dispatch + labor hours in advising drawee banks of delays in presentation	.293†
6.2 Percentage of cash letters not missent by courier error	Cost of dispatch	.077†
6.3 Percentage of cash letters not misfiled, mislabeled, or missent	Cost per 1,000 items for checks	-.024†
6.4 Percentage of outgoing cash letters not causing correspondence concerning misfiled, mislabeled, or missent cash letters	Cost of correcting + cost of dispatch + cost of preparation for dispatch	.480†
6.5 Dollar amount of adjustments required because of misfiled, mislabeled, and missent cash letters	Total dollars processing	.123†

Supplement D (continued)

Numerator	Denominator	Average Score
Deviation 7: Holdover (introduced in Demand, Receiving, and Preparation for Processing)		
7.1 Percentage of dollar volume received that does not become holdover	Cost of overtime scheduled to avoid holdover + cost of culling large dollar items	.347†
7.2 Percentage of dollar volume received that does not become holdover	Cost per 1,000 items for checks	-.310
7.3 Dollars holdover	Dollars volume received	.752†
7.4 Percentage of dollar volume received that becomes holdover	Percentage of dollar volume received that arrives during last hour	.767†

PART II
CONCEPTUAL MODELS FOR IMPROVEMENT

Along with measuring the quality dimension of productivity, a major question that again needs to be addressed in modeling productivity with an eye to improvement is that of the level in the economy that the modeling is to portray. Are we interested in productivity and quality modeling for a nation, an industry, a firm, the government, groups of employees, or individual workers? The answer to this question sets the stage for productivity modeling.

Two views seem to be paramount regarding productivity modeling: One is related to aggregate productivity for an industry or nation; the other is related to productivity within the organization. The first view has been presented by economists for decades; literature on economic productivity modeling and measurement is ubiquitous.

Our interest, however, lies not with the more aggregate productivity modeling and measurement issues of the economist but, rather, with productivity measurement and modeling <u>within</u> the organization. This book is directed toward organizational productivity with an emphasis on measuring quality of organization inputs and outputs. The focus is on the organization in total, the subfunction groupings of departments, and, to a lesser degree, the individual worker. We will examine individual productivity research that relates to quality. Our reason for doing so is to improve productivity measurement at the individual level. We are interested in individual productivity improvement, but we want first to assure good measures for tracking change. Subsequently, the department and entire organization measurement system should improve as individual and small-group performance is aggregated within the organization.

The models in Part II include both manufacturing and service sector applications. One reason for highlighting the service sector studies lies with the objectives of this book: to treat quality activities of a service function in either a manufacturing or a service industry. A second reason for stressing the service sector is that approximately two thirds of the work force is currently employed in the labor-intensive service sector of the U.S. economy. It is in this sector that productivity models focusing on behavioral factors--operative workers and administrators' behaviors --appear to hold the most promise as frameworks for productivity improvement programs.

We first present the productivity models that are general and descriptive (Chapter 5). General descriptive models include a productivity disaggregation model, an input-output model, Sutermeister's (1976) longstanding descriptive model of productivity and the factors affecting it, and a conceptual schematic model of factors affecting worker productivity.

Describing productivity and improving productivity are distinctly different issues. From the descriptive models emerge models for managing productivity (Chapter 6) with a focus on productivity improvement. A behavioral model by Lawler (1971) was selected to illustrate the type of modeling available for influencing behaviors toward more productive work. Additional literature dealing specifically with quality factors is briefly reviewed. A feedback (servo) model is provided to illustrate the contribution of systems theory to our understanding of productivity. Finally, a behavioral-technological model of factors affecting quality is presented. It is our belief that this behavioral-technological model has substantial potential for testing, subsequent revision, and useful application. The result could be a valuable tool for managers wanting to improve quality.

Several of these models have been developed by the authors. In such cases the reader should be able to associate parts of the developed model with literature and ideas of others in economics, the behavioral sciences, engineering, and systems theory. We do not want to imply that nonreferenced models are totally original. It seems to us that realistic modeling is a process of hypothesizing and empirical testing that has no distinct beginning and ending point. For complex issues such as quality and productivity modeling, we believe one would be rather naive to assume that all ideas are creative, making any one model "unique" in authorship.

The reader primarily interested in productivity and quality measurement may want to proceed directly to Part III, where measurement and improvement are related and several additional measurement applications are discussed. On the other hand, should the reader be interested in an abstract and conceptual presentation of productivity variables and their interrelationships, the following two chapters would be meaningful. The potential exists for some very practical applications once the models in Chapters 5 and 6 are understood.

5
General Descriptive Models

INTRODUCTION

The primary purpose of a productivity model is to provide a conceptual blueprint of the complex interrelationships and interactions of the many factors that influence the quantity and quality of product and service output. Conceptual models are necessarily less precise and less easily tested than are their physical counterparts; yet this should not be cause for omitting them from research efforts. Even an imprecise model aids in organizing thoughts, theories, and research results into a manageable set of interrelated concepts that can find practical applications in business firms.

A model can form the basis for intelligent discussion and debate concerning the factors and the relationships portrayed. It can serve to organize and classify existing research results to indicate which aspects of the model may be supported empirically and which remain to be tested. Finally, it can form a point of departure for the difficult tasks of theory development and hypothesis formulation and testing.

The four models presented in this chapter serve that purpose. The first, a disaggregation model, subdivides the inputs, outputs, and conversion technology along three orthogonal dimensions. Second, an input-output model of the firm shows the dynamic nature of combining inputs to form outputs to generate revenue that pays for additional inputs.

The last two models focus on factors affecting individual worker productivity. Sutermeister's model shows the relationships in the form of concentric circles around the core of productivity. The conceptual schematic model uses a modified tree diagram form to represent sequential levels of cause-and-effect or influencing relationships.

AN ORGANIZATIONAL PRODUCTIVITY DISAGGREGATION MODEL

Organizational productivity sometimes lends itself to disaggregation rather than to aggregation, the result being a family of productivity measures depending upon the attributes of productivity that interest management. A family of productivity measures may also be established by subdividing inputs, conversion technology, and outputs into useful subclasses. The rationale for selecting inputs and outputs as variables to be subdivided into classes is that these are the basic components of a productivity index. It is suggested that the conversion technology is an additional variable that is critical to productivity measurement, especially the disaggregation problem encountered in measurement. Although these seemed most critical after the literature review, there is no specific reason why other subdivisions might not lead to additional families of productivity measures.

Elements of the Model

Organizational productivity may be measured with families of productivity measures within any cell of the following matrix--a 4 x 4 x 2 matrix with four input variables, four conversion technologies, and two output characteristics (Figure 5-1). The inputs in the matrix are classical economic inputs; the outputs are quantity and quality dimensions of outputs used by production and

Figure 5-1 Organizational Productivity Disaggregation

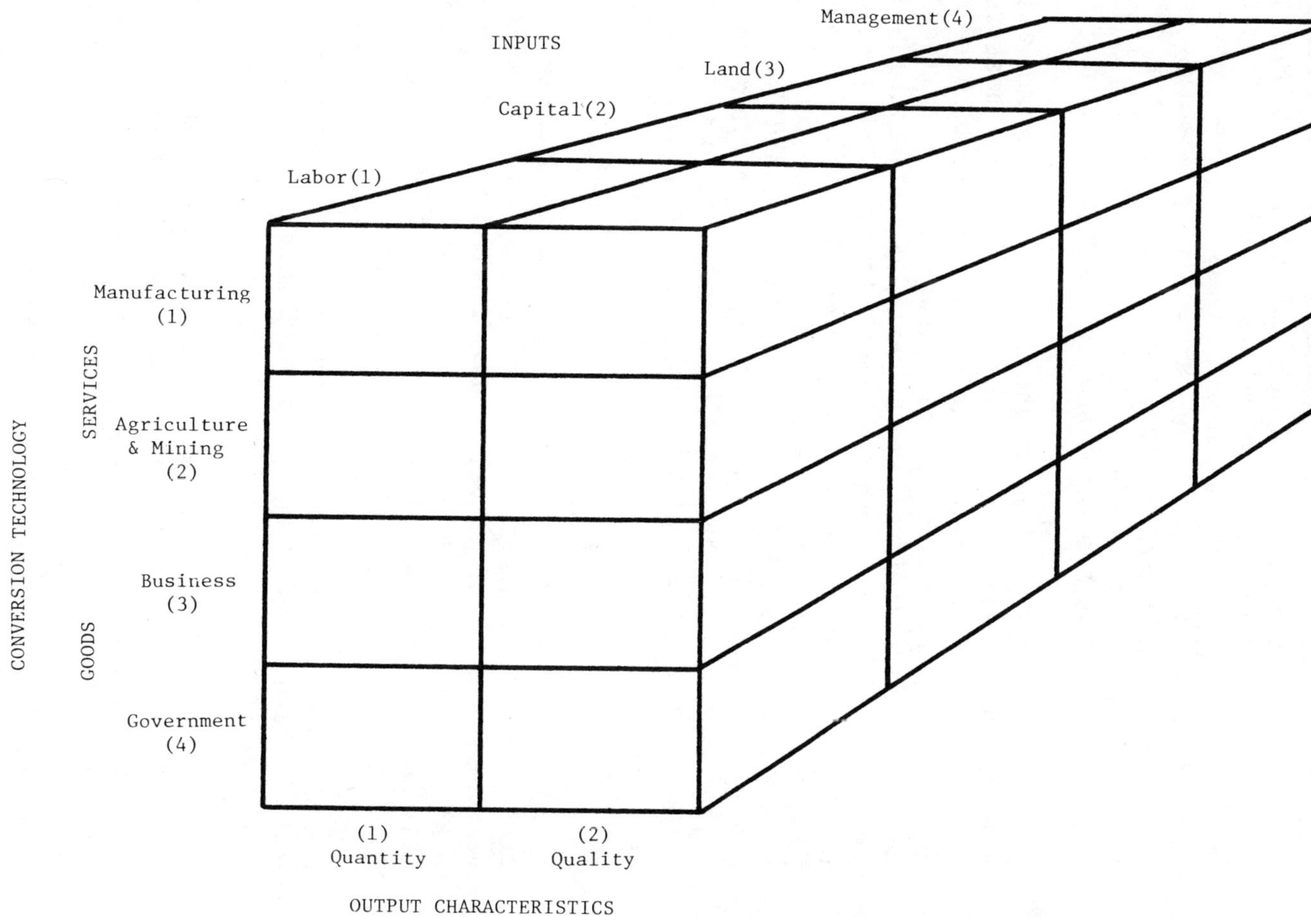

operations management; and the conversion technologies refer to the basic goods and services breakdowns used in government economic statistical data and were accepted on that basis. For an organization with a given conversion technology, a family of productivity measures may exist that utilizes various combinations of the four input and two output cells. Any one productivity index measures at least one input and at least one output.

It is likely that organizational productivity measures will result in different families of measures depending upon the level within the organization being measured. Thus the level of measurement is critical, be it at the individual, work group, department, plant, division, or higher organizational level. The productivity literature suggests that this is true. A set of productivity measurement indices focusing on individual output quantities, individual hours worked, and individual errors produced is quite different from plant labor efficiency, total plant hours worked, and plant scrap costs. The type of data employed in productivity measurement systems differs with varying organization levels.

At the present time, some measures exist at each of these levels; however, it is seldom possible to aggregate measures at one level to reach measures at the next higher level. If the ideal measurement scheme could be developed, measures could be aggregated or disaggregated by organizational level. Initial efforts toward this ideal have had little success; however, some progress is being made in developing productivity measures for various overhead functions such as purchasing and computer services (Ruch 1976).

Productivity measurement studies, measurement methods, and causal variable relationships with productivity are much more prevalent in manufacturing industries than in the service industries. They are especially absent, or nearly so, in government services. Quantity is the most common productivity dimension measured, often scaled on a cost basis. Quality is seldom measured as a dependent variable. An interpretation of the disaggregation model (Figure 5-1) suggests that productivity measurement sophistication varies across inputs from manufacturing (highest) to government (lowest) and from quantity (highest) to quality (lowest). This implies that, across inputs, the manufacturing-quantity cell would provide the most developed, sophisticated productivity measurement system whereas government service-quality productivity measurement systems would be least developed and sophisticated. Field research could be carried out to test this contention; however, additional questions arise as to whether this conclusion would hold if the term "productivity measurement system" were replaced with quantitative analysis, goal clarity, planning and control techniques, or similar management techniques and concepts and then field tested.

SOCIOTECHNICAL SYSTEMS AND DISAGGREGATION

Sociotechnical systems have been proposed as a method of viewing organizations (Davis and Taylor 1972), but the terms have not been widely accepted by academicians and practitioners. Yet, there can be application of the sociotechnical framework in studying productivity. The technical mapping literature is very helpful in assessing and measuring technology as it relates to productivity measures; in this regard, see Chase (1975), Engelstad (1972), Foster (1967), Herbst (1959), and Meissner (1969). Likewise, there are a multitude of psychological-sociological instruments to measure behavior and individual beliefs concerning the social aspects of productivity.

A general approach to productivity measurement is indicated. After acceptance of a general framework, such as the sociotechnical approach, specific items can be measured. For example, in goods producing conversion technologies, productivity measurement systems should measure a blend of technological and behavioral factors, whereas, for service conversion technologies, behaviors should be measured. For manufacturing, on the other hand, and to a slightly lesser extent for agriculture and mining, productivity measurement systems should assess the technological-behavioral characteristics of the inputs and outputs. Finally, for government, and to a slightly lesser extent for business services such as finance, entertainment, and medical delivery, productivity measurement systems should assess the behavioral characteristics much more heavily than the technological characteristics of inputs and outputs.

ATTITUDES, MOTIVATION, AND DISAGGREGATION

The experiences of Hostage (1975) at Marriott Hotels indicates that attitudes in a service industry are important, whereas Adam (1975) and Juran (1966) found the opposite to be the case for quality motivation programs in manufacturing. This suggests that attitudes and attitude measurement are much more critical components of productivity and productivity measurement for service conversion technologies than for goods producing conversion technologies. Further, sales managers who manage direct consumer contact technologies and long-term care administrators report that employee attitudes affect productivity substantially. Therefore, it is proposed that the closer the generation of a service (the conversion technology) is to the ultimate consumer of the outputs, the more critical attitudes and attitude measurement become to productivity and productivity measurement.

Finally, the most challenging productivity measurement situation and opportunity for subsequent improvement comes from a direct extension of the previous analysis. The least developed productivity measurement system across inputs seems to be measuring the quality dimension of productivity in government services. The productivity measurement focus in government services should be on behaviors. (Adam [1979] discussed this disaggregation model in more depth.) A review of related literature directs attention particularly to job characteristics, job design, instructions, worker attitudes, and contingency procedures. These behaviors involve both the labor and management cells of Figure 5-1.

Summary of the Organizational Productivity Disaggregation Model

The intent of this model is to show the relationship between productivity and the quality dimension of productivity to permit the development of a set of testable propositions. To do so, key terms were defined, and the literature concerning behavioral variables that relate to performance quality was reviewed. Measurement was an integral part of the discussion due to the lack of adequate productivity measurement systems. Productivity measurement systems historically have dealt primarily with quantity for the manufacturing sector at the worker or economy levels. This classification, however, subdivides the input variables, output characteristics, and conversion technologies to form a 4 x 4 x 2 matrix of combinations. Propositions were then formulated for some basic relationships. The classification, together with the propositions or interpretation, constitute the model.

Additional analysis could develop propositions and corollaries focusing on inputs rather than holding these inputs constant. To illustrate, productivity measurement would perhaps be most precise for land, then for capital and then direct labor, and least precise for management's contribution to productivity. The productivity literature indicates that measuring management's contribution to productivity, especially to the quality dimension of productivity, in government services is imprecise and presents a most challenging problem.

Once measurement systems are developed to deal with complete sets of factors, attention can be given to productivity improvement along the dimensions outlined by this model as well as others commonly addressed by those interested in productivity gains.

AN INPUT-OUTPUT MODEL OF THE FIRM

The purpose of this elementary model of the firm (Figure 5-2) is to emphasize that productivity, at the firm level, is a function of all of the various inputs to the production function and that, in turn, the firm's productivity is a major <u>determinant</u> of those inputs by providing the product or service to generate revenues that pay or reward the input factors. Viewed in this way, productivity is the pivotal point around which the firm, as a system, revolves.

This model focuses on productivity and enlarges it relative to the other factors in this system. It is a

Figure 5-2

An Input-Output Model of the Firm

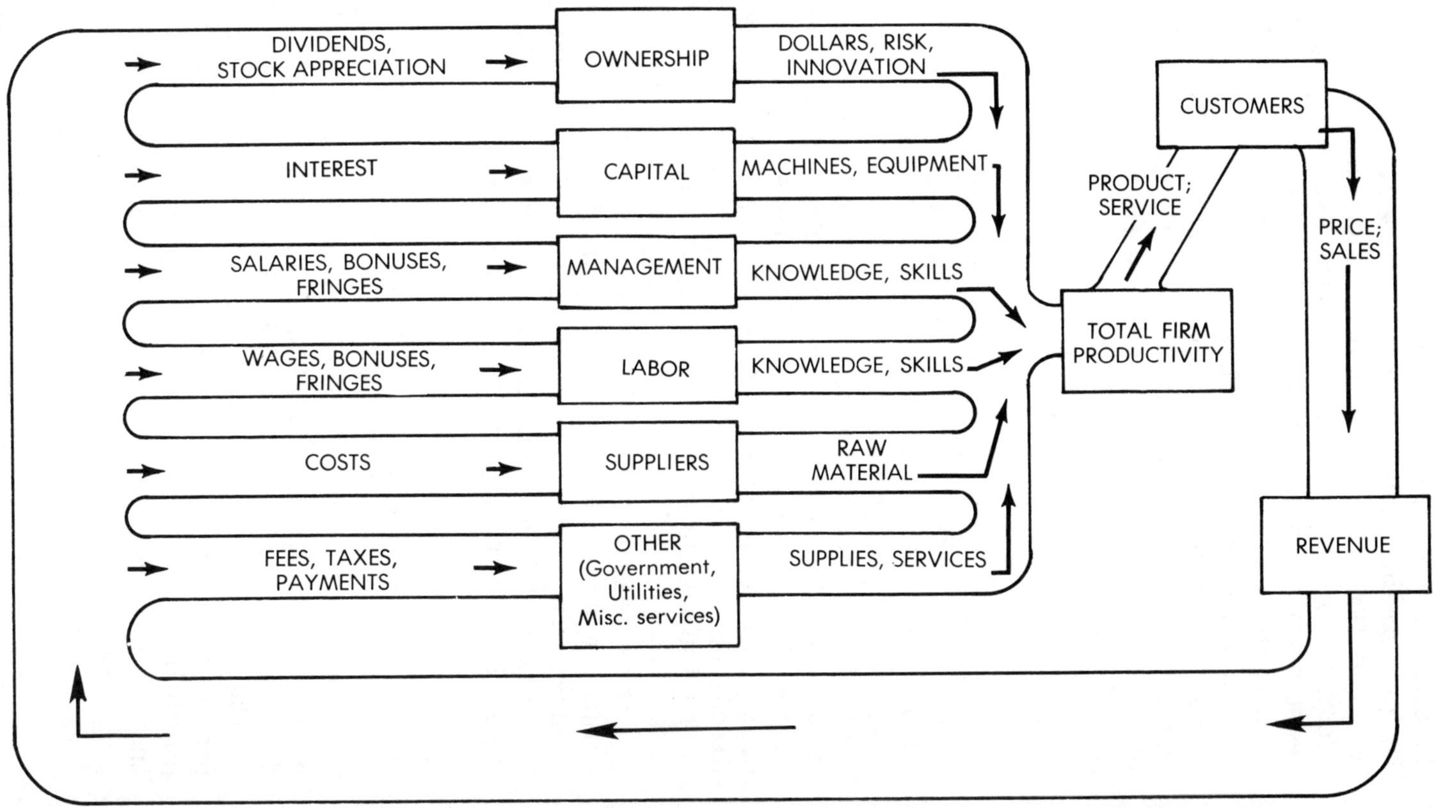

distorted view of the importance of productivity only if one accepts the narrow definition of productivity as referring to the output of direct operative labor. The broader definition of productivity at the firm level--the rate of conversion of inputs into all outputs--is adequately represented and properly emphasized in this model of the firm.

Peter Drucker recently said to be concerned exclusively with the productivity of the production worker is to look at only one factor. This leads to suboptimization--raising the productivity of the worker at the cost of (less productivity of) capital, land, and physical resources. What is needed is a systems approach to include all factors.[1] This model is designed to focus attention on all of the inputs to the firm's productivity and thereby instigate the development of a systems way of thinking about productivity.

Six sources of inputs to the firm are identified and the general nature of the input from each is shown. These factors of production are combined in some way within the box labeled total firm productivity. No attempt is made in this model to indicate _how_ those inputs are converted into goods and services. The purpose is to emphasize that output is a function of all of these factors and that productivity is a function of both the level of the inputs and the way in which they are combined.

The output of the firm flows to the customer where it is converted to dollars of revenue for the firm as determined by price and demand. The revenue then becomes a payment for each of the inputs to the firm, and the process recycles.

The firm may change the absolute or the relative level of the input factors, thereby changing the level of output even though the efficiency of combining those

---

[1]Peter F. Drucker, "Beyond Efficiency to Effectiveness." Speech given to the Spring Conference of Work Factor Associates of the West, Anaheim, California, May 3, 1974. (Paraphrased, as no text of the speech is available.)

inputs has not changed. For example, a new piece of capital equipment may be installed (perhaps combined with a reduction in labor) to cause an increase in output. If demand permits, this will result in an increase in revenue sufficient to at least cover the cost of the additional capital. The change, it is hoped, will generate enough revenue to also increase the flow of funds to the owners of the firm. If labor is reduced as a part of the change, payment to this factor is correspondingly reduced.

Sometimes changes occur that are outside the control of the firm. For example, an increase in the interest rates on capital will make capital more expensive relative to labor. The result should be a change toward a more labor-intensive process in an effort to return the system to equilibrium. Exactly the opposite would occur if the initial change were an increase in wages or some other payment to labor. Similar statements can be made for any of the inputs: an exogenous change in one will require some change in the network to return the system to equilibrium. It should be noted, however, that the ownership factor is often the residual in the sense that it seldom has the power to demand higher payment for its inputs; it must accept what remains after the other inputs are covered.

Changing the absolute or relative level of the inputs is only one way in which to return the system to equilibrium. A second way is by adjusting the price of the output. If demand will permit, an increase in the cost of some input, say, in the cost of raw materials, can be passed along to the customer through an increase in price. Thus, if the model is viewed as a hydraulic network, price can be interpreted as an adjustment valve to balance the flow of output and dollars just as each of the inputs has an adjusting valve to control the flow of that input into the system.

Another major adjusting valve--one that is often overlooked--is productivity. If the cost of an input increases and demand in the marketplace does not permit adjustment of the price valve, the firm may have to "work smarter" if it is to avoid a decrease in the payments to the ownership of the firm. Working smarter means a better, more efficient way of combining the inputs to create more output with the same, or even less, inputs. In other words, the firm can attempt to increase its productivity.

If productivity is increased in direct response to cost pressures from some input, the additional funds generated may be directed exclusively to that input. However, the real world is seldom that simple; many changes are taking place simultaneously, and the system is generally in a state of dynamic disequilibrium making adjustments in an effort to achieve a better balance. Thus, when a productivity gain is achieved, it is sometimes difficult to isolate the direct cause of the change and to recompense one input factor. Of the input groups, ownership and labor are both likely to claim credit for the productivity gain and feel that they deserve the benefits from it.

This issue--the equitable division of the benefits of productivity gains among owners, management, and labor--is at the heart of many labor disputes and has formed the basis for many profit sharing plans now in existence. This model will not solve that dispute, but it may serve to clarify the nature of the dispute by diagraming the part that each factor plays in the productivity of the firm and by establishing that each has a legitimate claim to the returns from productivity gains.

Although this model provides some insights to productivity as an integral part of an input-output analysis of the firm, it leaves a great deal unsaid by representing productivity as a "black box." The purpose of the next two models is to look into that "black box" and examine the way in which many individual and organizational factors impact on the productivity of the individual worker.

SUTERMEISTER'S MODEL OF WORKER PRODUCTIVITY

Relatively few models of performance exist that attempt to explain the interrelationships of factors influencing worker productivity. Sutermeister (1976) presents a comprehensive descriptive model, however, in his book <u>People and Productivity</u>. The model (Figure 5-3) is a series of concentric circles surrounding

Figure 5-3

Sutermeister's Model: Major Factors Affecting Employees' Job Performance and Productivity

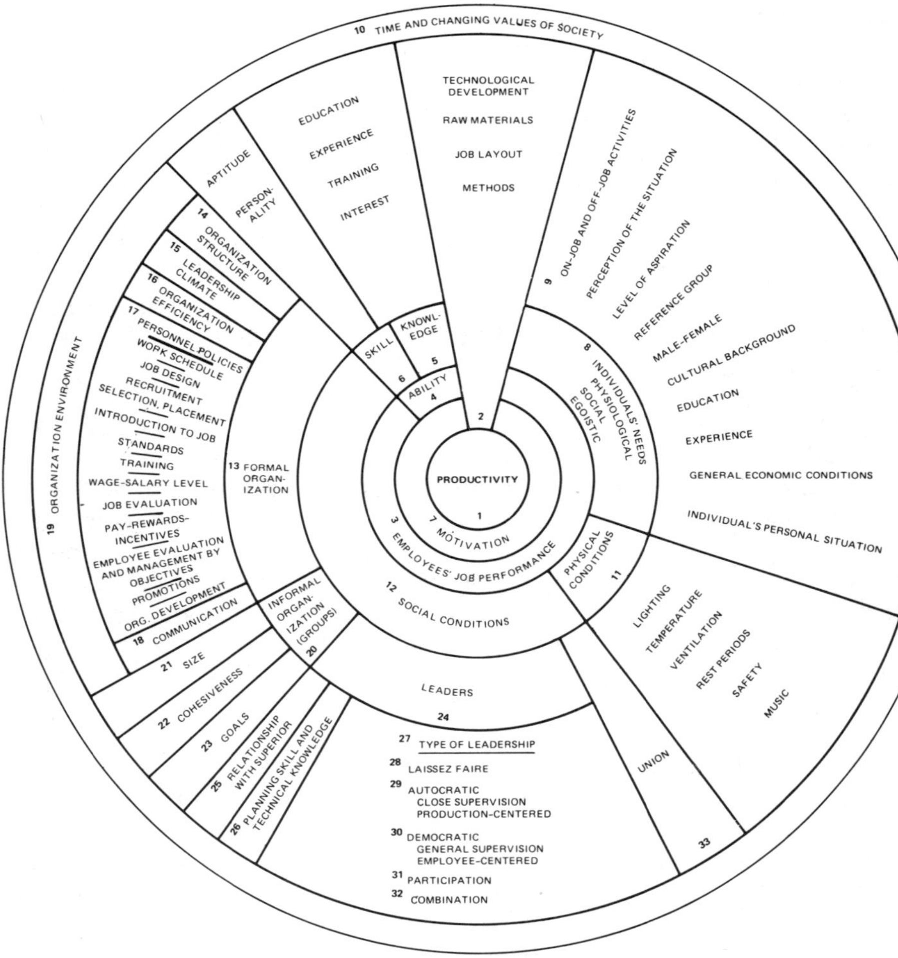

1. The size of each segment has no relationship to its relative importance, which would vary with different organizations, different departments, and even different individuals with their own distinct needs.
2. The factors in each segment affect factors in the corresponding segment of the next smaller circle; they may also affect and be affected by other segments in the same circle or other circles.
3. The numbers in the various sections of the diagram correspond to figures in parentheses throughout Chapters 1 to 18.

productivity with factors closer to the center being more direct in their influence on productivity.

Sutermeister's definition of productivity includes quality:

> When 20 units were produced by one person in one hour last month and 22 identical units are produced by one person in one hour today, productivity has risen ten percent. If 20 units were produced last month and 20 units of higher quality are produced today, productivity has also risen, although the measurement of it is more difficult. (Sutermeister 1976, p. 5)

The model first divides all factors into two groups: technological development and employee motivation. The role of technology in determining productivity will vary greatly across industries, but its management is relatively straightforward. The remainder of the model explores the motivation factor. Motivation is a function of ability and employees' job performance. Ability, in turn, is composed of skill and knowledge, whereas job performance is influenced by the individuals' needs and the physical and social conditions of the workplace. Additional relationships are found by traveling outward through successive segments of the concentric circles.

In his explanation of the model, Sutermeister emphasizes the complexity of the interrelationships of the factors:

> It is possible . . . for individuals' needs to be pretty well met, for them to be fairly well satisfied with job and firm, and for them to have a fairly high level of morale but to willfully restrict their output, not to perform at their best, and in effect work against the company goal of increased productivity. The relation between need satisfaction, morale, employees' job performance, and productivity is much too complex for us to assume that satisfaction of individuals' needs will automatically lead to better job performance and increased productivity. (Sutermeister 1976, p. 12)

Sutermeister's model provides an excellent overview of the many factors involved in productivity improvement. The next model places some of these same factors in a format to indicate causal or influential relationships.

A CONCEPTUAL SCHEMATIC MODEL OF FACTORS AFFECTING INDIVIDUAL WORKER PRODUCTIVITY

Viewing productivity as a function of many inputs led to the formulation of the conceptual schematic model of factors affecting worker productivity (Figure 5-4). This model incorporates the major factors, both organizational and extraorganizational, that have a direct causal effect on the productivity of the individual worker. The orientation of this model is primarily toward the operative worker; however, it can be generalized to nonoperative workers through the redefinition of some terms and the elimination of some factors that may not apply to jobs in which no physical product is involved. Generalization to technical or managerial positions is not intended from the model as formulated.

Major factors in this model of productivity are represented by rectangles, and direct effects between factors (causal or strongly influential) are indicated by solid arrows. Circles are used to denote factors that act as filters or buffers within the influential relationship between two major factors. Bodies of knowledge from which the organization draws are contained in irregular figures. Causal or influential effects, which are weaker but nevertheless important, are indicated in the model as dotted-line arrows.

Using the Model

Productivity is a function of three primary factors: the capacity of the task, the individual effort brought by the worker to the task, and interference that cannot be controlled by the individual. These three factors are combined through some form of work measurement to yield productivity data for the individual for some specified time period.

Figure 5–4

A Conceptual Schematic Model of Factors Affecting Worker Productivity

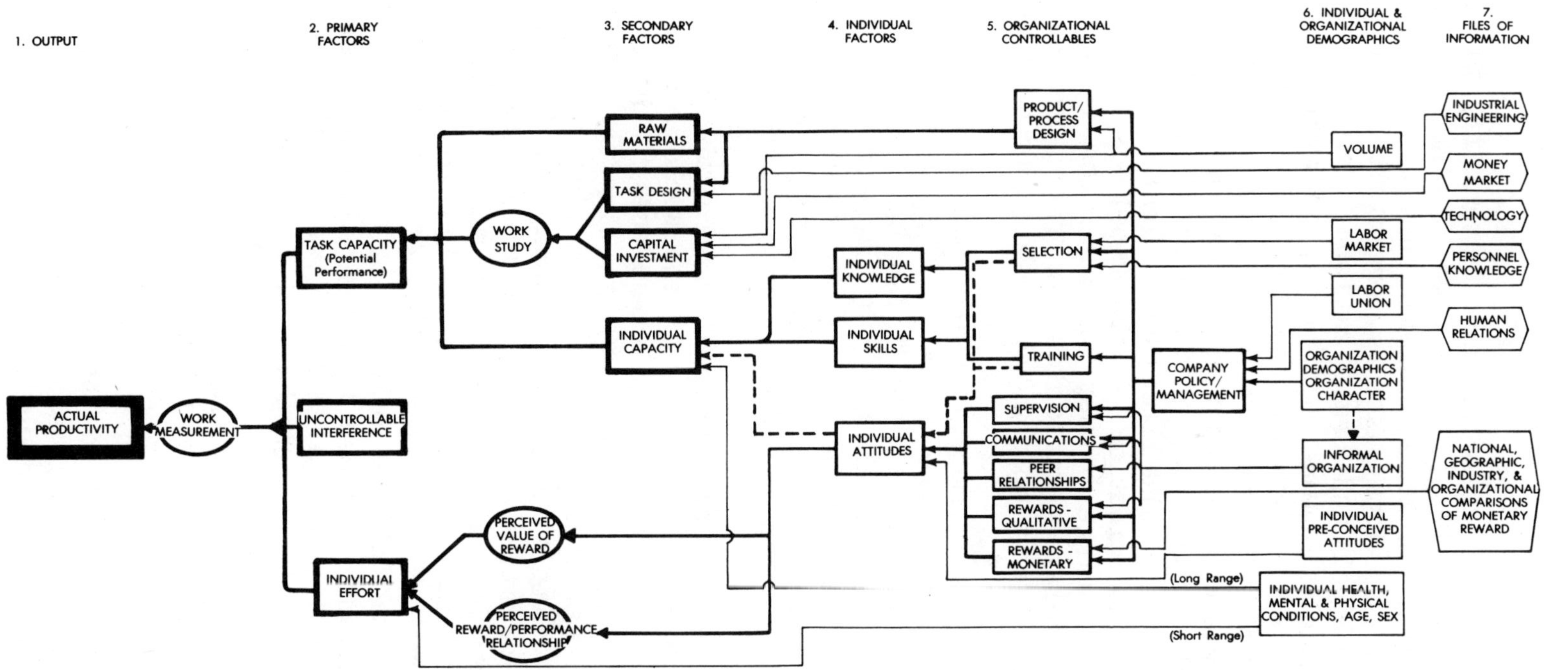

Each of these primary factors is, in turn, determined or strongly influenced by other factors, and the chain of relationships continues through secondary factors, individual factors, organizational controllables, individual and organizational demographics (uncontrollable in the short run), and, finally, bodies or files of information and knowledge relating to productivity. The factors included in this model and their effects upon one another are not new to most students of productivity; most of the elements of this diagram are supported in the literature. The unique aspect--and the major contribution of the model--is the combining of such a large number of variables into a system of interrelated variables comprehensive enough to be useful, yet simple enough to be comprehensible.

As an example, consider the factors of individual attitudes. The attitude of the individual worker concerning work itself, the company for which he or she works, his or her job, pay, and so on, is a major determinant of the effort that worker brings to the task contingent upon his or her perceptions of the rewards from the job and the relationship between rewards and performance. These individual attitudes are a function of several organizational controllables as well as the preconceived attitudes of the worker, formed in childhood and earlier work experiences. The organizational controllables, which impinge directly on the individual's attitude, may be a function of company policy. For example, monetary rewards are determined by the organization with consideration given to national, geographic, and industrial averages for the type of job. Other factors influencing individual attitudes are determined by a combination of company policy and the influence of the informal organization. The relative importance of these antecedents on supervision, communications, and qualitative rewards will differ from one organization to another and from time to time within a given organization. One of the factors--peer relationships--is organizational but is determined almost exclusively by the informal organization rather than by company policy.

In addition to these primary determinants of individual attitudes, some influence can be exerted by the organization through training and selection. This relationship is not as strong, primarily because of the difficulty in accurately measuring attitudes and a lack of knowledge of the nature of the relationship between specific, identifiable attitudes and the worker's productivity.

The indication of a direct causal or influential relationship between any two factors in this model is intended to indicate a substantial agreement among students of productivity that such a relationship exists; however, it is not necessarily true that empirically based knowledge is available to explain the precise nature of that relationship. There is a wealth of knowledge in industrial engineering, for example, on the factors determining the capacity of the task. But there is a great need for more information to support and explain the effect of the informal organization on peer relationships and the subsequent effect upon individual attitudes toward work.

Interactions Among Factors

In addition to the obvious interactions between two or more factors that jointly determine a factor, there are some interactions within the schematic that deserve special note. First, consider the interaction of the task design with several other factors in the schematic. Task design interacts with individual attitudes in the sense that each is influenced by the other but neither one directly determines the other. If the task design is inherently inefficient, clumsy, and displeasing to the individual, the person may exert less effort than he or she would in a more satisfying task. On the other hand, if a task is so streamlined, specified, and standardized that it is dehumanized, the individual may rebel from the job by withdrawing some of the effort that he or she might otherwise put into it. In fact, the worker may turn to dysfunctional activities. The task design may also interact with the peer relationships in some cases. Designing tasks as a moving assembly line can change the effect on the individual of peer relationships. Tasks that are group oriented and designed to be interdependent in process tend also to cause the workers of the group to become interdependent socially; in this case the peer relationships would be extremely strong in determining actual productivity.

Task design can also interact with supervision. Tasks that are not well designed or tasks that allow the individual freedom of choice may require closer supervision than will tasks that are more routine. Therefore, the number of people that a supervisor is able to supervise may depend partly upon the way in which the tasks are designed.

Trade-offs

Trade-offs exist at several points in the schematic, for example, among secpondary factors--raw materials, task design, capital investment, and individual capacity. A greater investment in capital equipment in the form of a labor-saving machine may mean that less is required in the way of task design and possibly less is required in the way of raw materials.

Another major trade-off is the trade-off between selection and training. Skills and knowledge that cannot be found in the labor market may have to be developed within the firm.

Another major trade-off exists between the qualitative (i.e., nonmonetary rewards) and the monetary rewards. The critical issue in many incentive pay systems, for example, is how much to pay to the individual in cash and how much to retain in the form of company benefits such as retirement funds or some other less immediate reward for the worker.

Feedback

Since actual productivity is the ultimate goal of this particular model, the major feedbacks will be from productivity back to one of the factors that determines productivity. The most obvious example of this is from productivity back to both monetary and qualitative rewards. In the case of a piecework pay system, profit sharing, or other incentive pay system, such feedback is well established and an integral part of the operation of the firm. In cases in which workers are not paid on an incentive basis, such feedback may come in a less structured fashion and over longer periods of time for purposes of periodic review and increases in pay. Often, qualitative rewards are given on the basis of productivity. For example, an individual may be selected worker of the month and have his or her picture in the company house organ for exceeding a production quota.

A second major feedback loop from productivity would go to company policy. Company policy is often formulated on the basis of past successes and failures. If success and failure are measured to some extent in terms of productivity, then productivity becomes an input to a decision to make changes in company policy or to a confirmation that current company policy should be continued.

Summary of the Conceptual Schematic Model

The schematic presented in Figure 5-4 is a simplistic model of a highly complex system of interrelated factors that influence individual worker productivity. A major effort has been made to limit the model to only those factors that appear to have a major impact upon productivity and those factors and interactions about which some research-based knowledge has been developed.

It would be easy to double or triple the number of factors listed here and still make a good case for them as additional influences on productivity. Similarly, it would be easy to draw a deterministic relationship from any one factor to almost any other factor and find some justification for it after the fact. This is true also about feedback loops, trade-offs, and interactions. The result of such a model, however, would explain no more about the area of productivity than is already known: It is extremely complex. Nor would the resulting model be of much benefit in organizing the known information about productivity.

The model presented here is sufficiently comprehensive to provide a framework for much of the research that has been done concerning productivity. For example, consider a research study into the effects of nonmonetary awards on individual attitudes. It can be seen from the schematic where this fits into the general order of things, and the way in which influencing the individual's attitude will eventually influence the actual productivity of the form. As information is thus cataloged, areas within the schematic that have been the subject of little or no research begin to be discernible.

SUMMARY

It has been established that productivity is a highly complex subject, that it is caused or influenced by a multiplicity of interrelated factors, and that it suffers from the misconceptions and misunderstandings associated with a variety of vague and misleading definitions and measurement formulas. It is unlikely, therefore, that any one model or theory will emerge that will explain productivity in all of its complexity at the national, organizational, and individual worker levels. No such claim is made for any of the models presented in this chapter.

These models range from the very general disaggregation model to models of specific aspects of individual worker productivity. The organizational productivity disaggregation model (Figure 5-1) delineated four inputs and four conversion technologies as they relate to quantity and quality of output to form a framework for separating different situations for productivity analysis. The input-output model of the firm (Figure 5-2) took a systems appoach to productivity by emphasizing that total firm productivity is a function of all of the inputs to the firm, their absolute and their relative levels, and the way in which they are combined to yield salable outputs.

Sutermeister's model (Figure 5-3) provided an array of factors that influence productivity and provided some insights into their complex interactions. The conceptual schematic model of factors affecting worker productivity (Figure 5-4) examined productivity in more detail, showing some of the more important influential relationships and leading to recognition of interactions, trade-offs, and feedback.

Whereas the models in this chapter lead to conceptual understanding, the models in Chapter 6 are more prescriptive. They begin to bridge the gap between understanding the problem and taking positive action toward solution.

6
Models for Managing Improvements

INTRODUCTION

The models presented in Chapter 5 were descriptive. The intent of descriptive models is to enumerate factors involved in productivity. In this chapter, we present models that identify the nature of factor interactions and the direction of influence. Specification of mathematical functions and parameters could be done; however, precise mathematical relationships would be purely speculative, as measurement and management theory have not developed to the point of known definitive relationships.

An often discussed and used normative behavioral model related to performance is Lawler's motivational model. Lawler suggests probabilistic relationships with feedback loops in an attempt to explain performance. It is presented here as a lead-in to the two productivity models that follow.

Whereas Sutermeister's model is descriptive of the many physical, individual, and social variables that affect worker productivity, Lawler's motivation model is a normative model of individual performance. Although dealing with fewer factors, Lawler attempts to explain the direction and relative magnitude of performance changes. The model emphasizes the relationships among psychological preset, equity perceptions, satisfaction, and ability in affecting effort and effort-to-performance probabilities. Figure 6-1 (Lawler 1971) shows the nature of these psychological relationships and performance.

A NORMATIVE PRODUCTIVITY MODEL

Consistent with our definition of productivity in Chapter 1, organization productivity relates outputs to inputs through a conversion process. The servosystem model of worker productivity, depicted in Figure 6-2, represents this conversion process for operative employees. It is based on existing literature and from information gathered during analysis of several productivity-conscious organizations (Ruch and Hershauer 1974). The models by Lawler and Sutermeister were particularly useful in forming the model. In addition to these two models that have been discussed in this book, the modeling procedures of industrial dynamics, as developed by Forrester (1961), guided the form used. Much of the discussion that follows is directly from an article in Interfaces (Hershauer and Ruch 1978).

Structure of the Model

The model has been kept at a level of detail that, it is hoped, maintains both conceptual meaning and practical utility. Individual worker performance is shown as the focal point of the model; organizational and individual factors either directly or indirectly impact this performance. Any factor shown in the model can be traced through the model as an input to worker performance. In fact, many factors also can be traced to performance as an output. Because of this feedback effect and the time delay characteristics, the model has been labeled a "servosystem," that is, a dynamic feedback system. As stated by Roberts (1975, p. 1), "A dynamic feedback system is an ongoing set of relationships in which the output of an action taken by one person or group eventually has an effect again on that person or group."

Figure 6-1

Lawler's Motivational Model

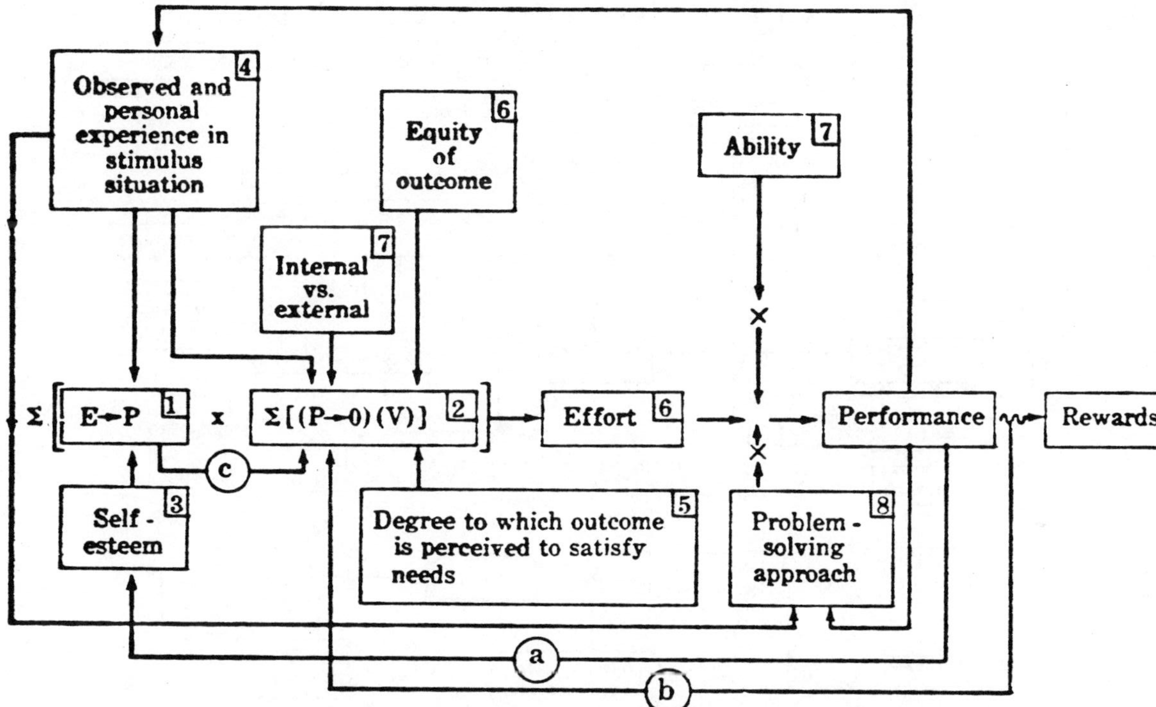

Lawler, Edward E., Pay and Organizational Effectiveness: A Psychological View. New York: McGraw-Hill, 1971, p. 108.

Figure 6–2

Servosystem Model of Worker Productivity

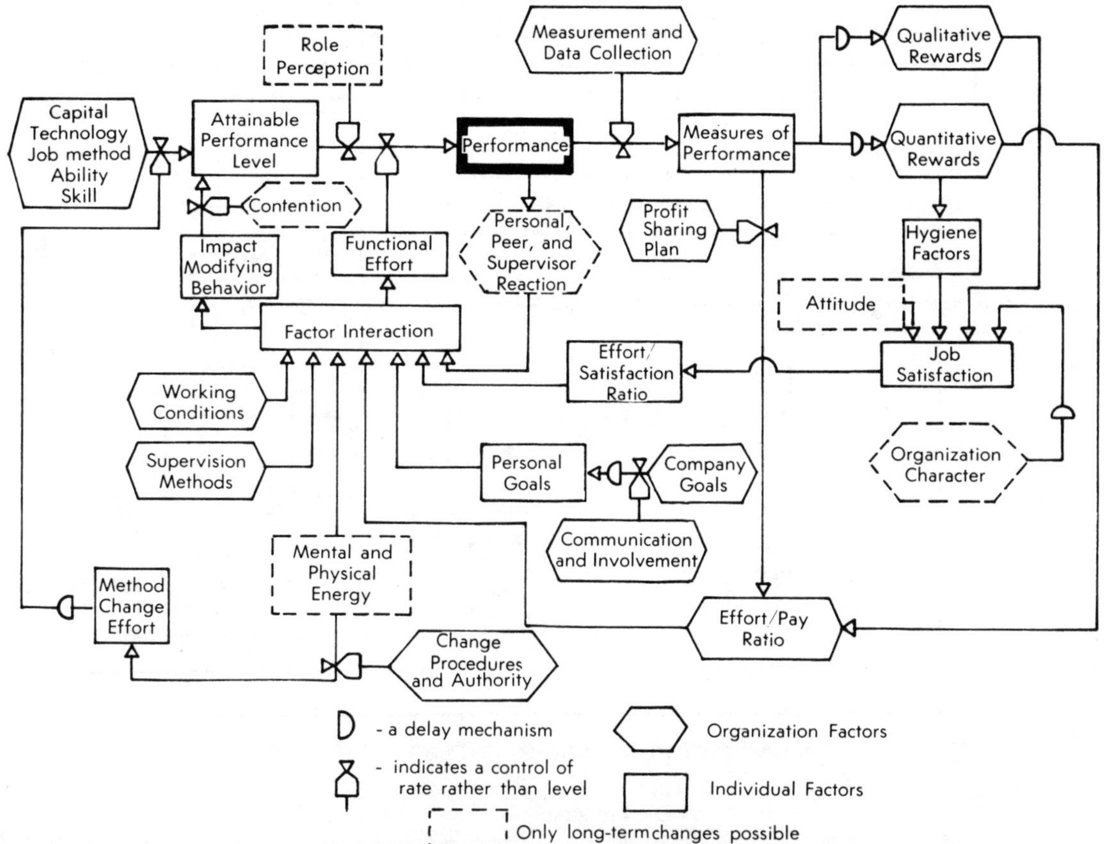

Factors are indicated in the model in several different ways. First, individually controlled factors are distinguished from organizationally controlled factors by differently shaped figures. Second, factors that may be changed significantly only in the long run are identified separately by dotted-line figures. Third, some factors serve to control the rate of transfer of one or more of the other variables. Fourth, the model includes time as an implicit factor, since the feedback would take place over time. The time factor is also explicitly included by the time delays shown at a variety of places in the model. These delays indicate that changes in the factors to which they relate will affect performance gradually over time. Fifth, the "factor interaction" block indicates that "functional effort" of individuals is a complex phenomenon that is more than a simple addition of the levels of the factors that are direct inputs of the individual.

Model Description

In the figures that follow, each significant portion of the model is explained separately. It is important to note that these are only parts of the total model; they do not stand on their own. Once understood, they must be integrated into the total model depicted in Figure 6-2.

Figure 6-3 indicates that there are basically two ways in which to obtain performance. First, a potential for each job exists as an attainable performance level. Second, the functional effort exerted by an individual determines what portion of the attainable is achieved.

Figure 6-3 also concentrates on one factor influencing functional effort: personal, peer, and supervisor reaction. Worker performance leads to some reaction from both peers and supervisors and also leads to an internal reaction by the worker himself or herself in the form of pride, shame, indifference, or some other feeling. These reactions become a part of the factor interaction that results in functional effort. A common example of this phenomenon is the problem with rate busting that exists in many organizations. Standard performance set by the company may not be achieved because workers have decided, within informal groups,

Figure 6-3

Central Model Factors

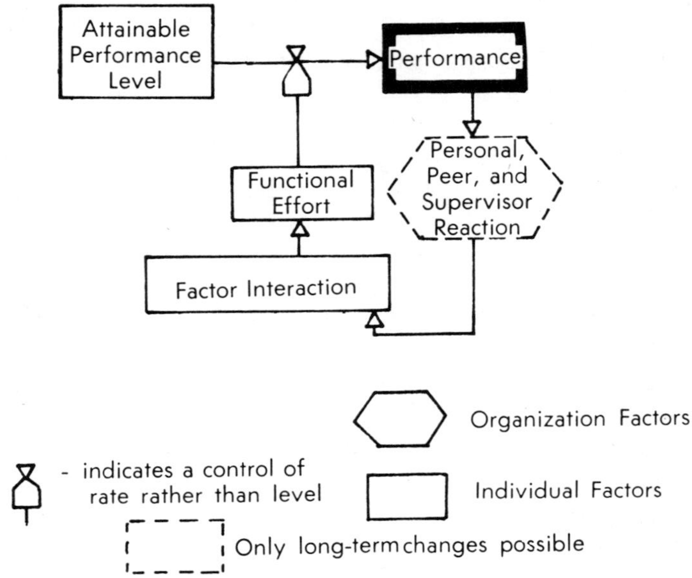

that the standard is unfair. They can set their own lower standard and are able to enforce conformity through the creative use of peer pressure on the new employee who attempts to reach the organizational goal.

Figure 6-4 centers on the mental and physical energy of the worker and how this energy is employed in the organization. Typically, most of the worker's energy flows through the factor interaction to become functional effort directed toward performance.

In some organizations, however, emphasis is placed on working smarter rather than working harder. This occurs when an explicit program exists that encourages changes in the methods and procedures for performing the work. Thus, a worker may devote some fraction of his or her mental and physical energy to method change effort that should help to determine a better way to perform the job rather than simply using that time and energy to produce a few more units. This allows the resources of the organization to be employed more efficiently and effectively and raises the attainable performance level for the task. Thus, organizations may control

Figure 6-4

Worker Energy and Technology

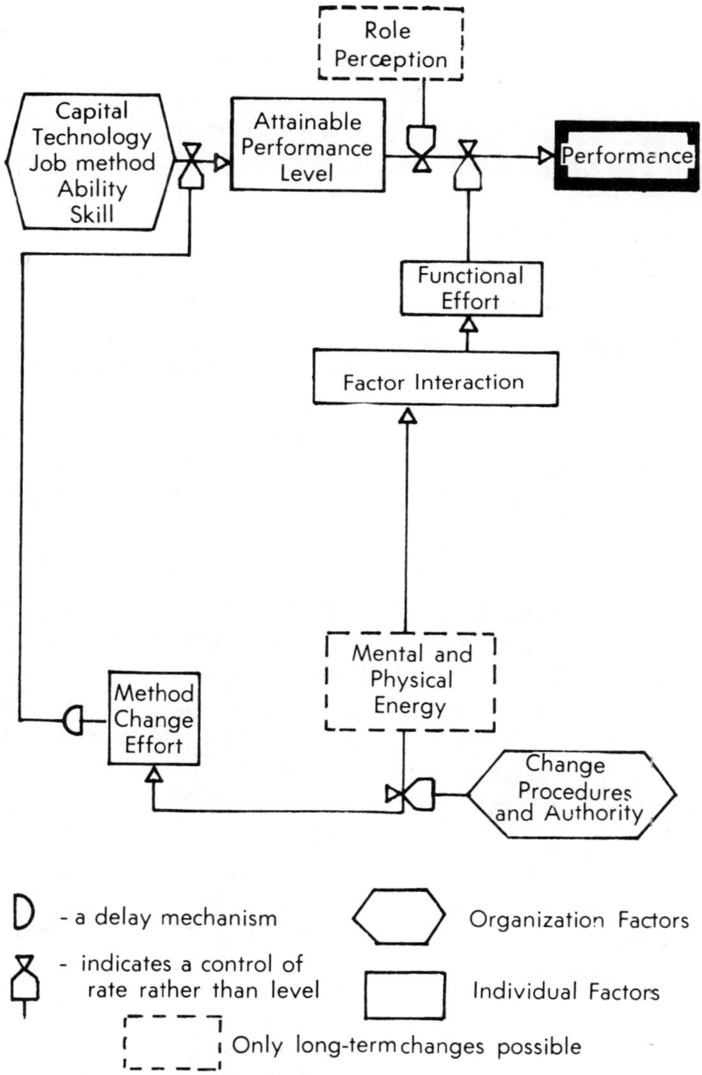

attainable performance levels through change procedures and authority as well as through the normal investments in capital, technology, job method, ability, and skill.

An individual variable that intercedes between attainable performance level and functional effort is also shown in Figure 6-4. An improper role perception on the part of an individual worker may cause his or her functional effort to be devoted toward an improper objective and result in poor performance regarding desired objectives.

Figure 6-5 addresses performance. True performance leads to measures of performance--measures that are as accurate or as inaccurate as the measurement and data collection system employed. Measures of performance, in turn, lead to qualitative (nonmonetary) rewards and quantitative (monetary) rewards. Both types of rewards have important influences on the individual's job satisfaction.

Job satisfaction leads to an individual factor, the effort-satisfaction ratio. This factor represents the amount of effort an individual is willing to expend for different levels of satisfaction. Different individuals, of course, could have vastly different effort-satisfaction ratios. In addition to being a determinant of job satisfaction, quantitative rewards also lead to the effort-pay ratio. This organizational factor indicates the amount of pay that the organization considers commensurate with a given level of effort--a concept reflecting the notion of a fair day's work for a fair day's pay.

Both of these effort ratios lead to the critical factor interaction box. Here the effort ratios interact with other factors in some complex way to yield the functional effort of the individual at his or her job. If that functional effort is normal, then the attainable performance level will be achieved in actual performance. If effort is less than normal, actual performance will fall short of what is possible. At this point, we have come full circle and the feedback cycle is ready to begin again.

Figure 6-5

Performance Feedback Factors

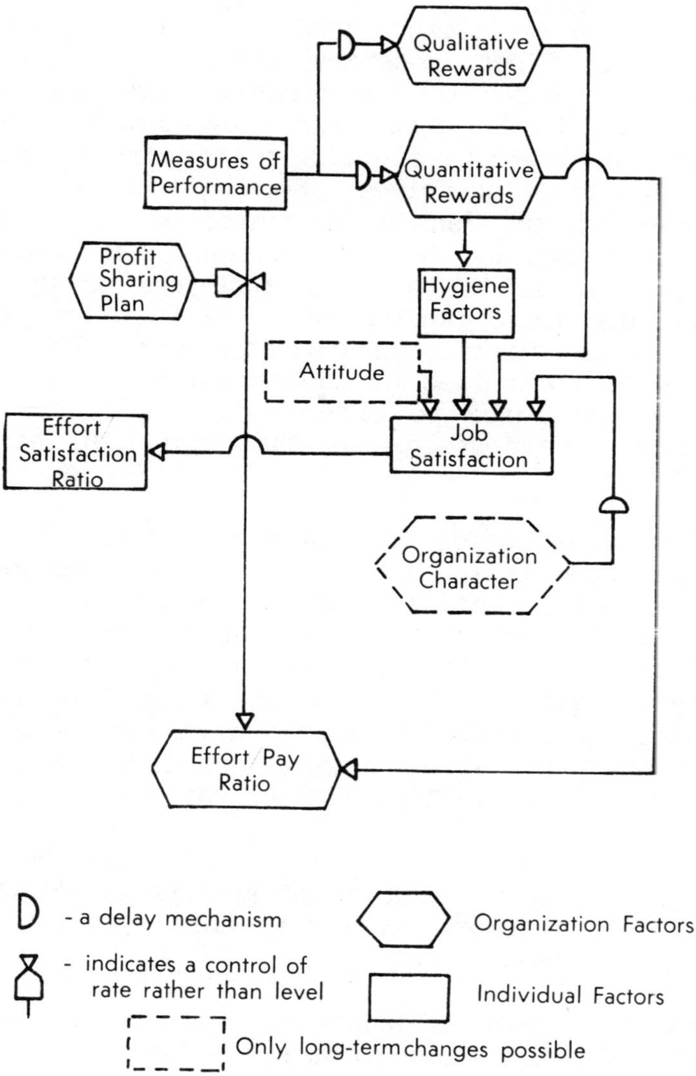

Figure 6-6 is used to highlight those variables whose impact on functional effort is fed back through the effort-satisfaction and effort-pay ratios.

Measures of performance lead to the effort-pay ratio in two ways. First, monetary payment is reflected in quantitative rewards through programs regarding salary, hourly rate, direct bonus for above-standard performance, pay increments reflecting performance relative to others, and price incentives. Second, there is a direct link whose rate of transfer is controlled by the profit sharing plan used by the organization. The concept of profit sharing is to have all employees share in any improvements in organizational savings or profits immediately and directly in a known manner. The effort-pay ratio is controlled by the organization. However, employees are quick to discover any discrepancies, inequalities, or inadequacies that exist in the ratio structure.

Effort-satisfaction is a more nebulous and complex ratio controlled by the individual worker based upon his or her job satisfaction. Job satisfaction level is strongly influenced in the long run by the attitude of the individual and the organization character. In the short run, hygiene factors that the individual can purchase with quantitative rewards provided and motivation created by qualitative rewards received can cause fluctuations in an individual's job satisfaction.

In most of the previous partial diagrams the factor interaction block has been an integral part. Figure 6-7 highlights the factors comprising this interaction and its immediate results.

There is strong evidence for linking each of the interacting factors shown to worker peformance; however, the synergistic effect of combining them in a specific mix is not well understood. Typically, each factor is studied, analyzed, and changed separately with additive combinatorial effects being assumed. This model makes no simplistic assumption, but neither does it propose the specific nature of the interactions.

In addition to previously discussed variables, two others--working conditions and personal goals--have a

Figure 6-6

Effort Ratios

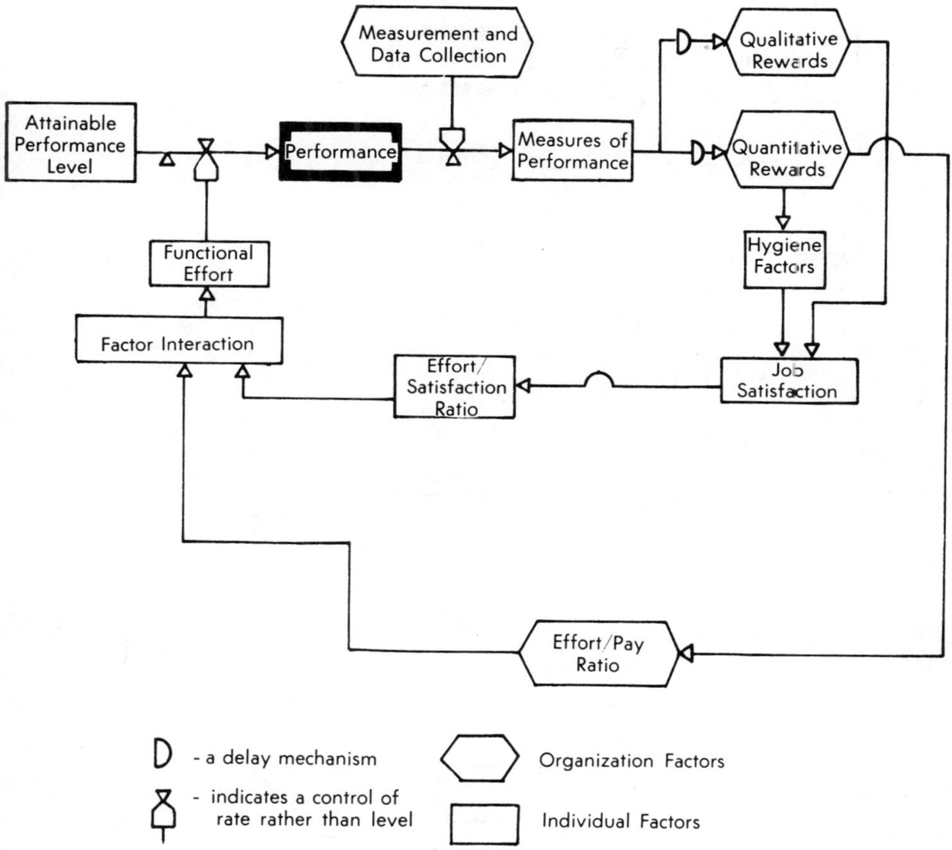

Figure 6–7

Factor Interaction

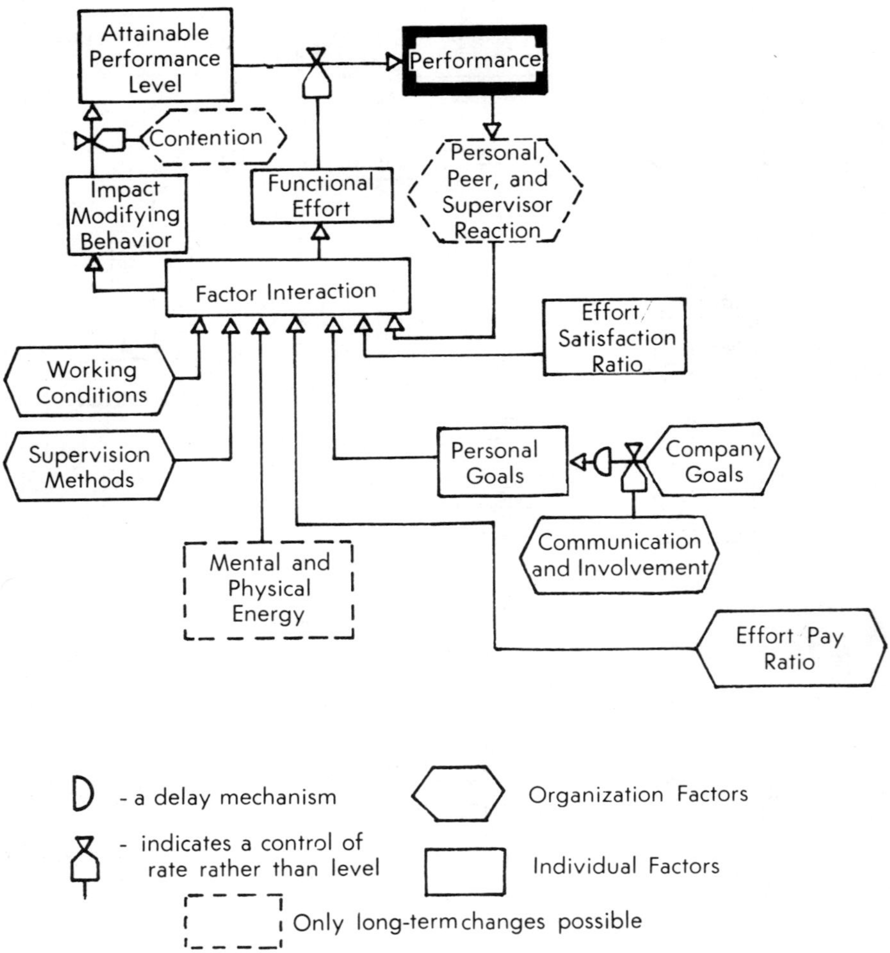

direct bearing on the functional effort of the individual. Personal goals will relate back to company goals to the extent that communication and involvement characterize management philosophy. The congruence of personal and company goals largely determines the functional nature of personal effort, whereas the other six variables entering the factor interaction block primarily determine level of effort.

The result of the factor interaction may be functional effort--effort expended on the task in organizationally acceptable ways. An alternative, however, is for the worker to engage in some impact-modifying behavior (often to relieve the boredom of a routine or distasteful job) and engage in nonproductive or even antiproductive acts. This impact-modifying behavior, controlled partly by the degree of contention between labor and management, may reduce the attainable performance level by disrupting the flow of work, destroying company resources, losing time, or a host of other variations.

The completed model has been well received and is becoming well used. Lincoln Electric, for one, uses the worker productivity model as a training tool for front-line supervisors. Management felt that the model properly described the company's operating philosophy and, thus, should be understood by all supervisors. One supervisor, in each of three departments, was given the model to study. At the next supervisors' meeting, these individuals were asked to present and explain their analysis of the model to their peers. Hearing the presentation from fellow supervisors, rather than from a top manager, ensured more effective communication of the ideas in the model and enhanced its chances for acceptance and implementation.

George E. Willis, president of Lincoln Electric, informed us of the following results, based upon their use of the model:

1. When the supervisors presented the model to their peers, it was obvious that they had attained a better understanding of the complexity of their jobs and the interrelationships and tradeoffs that lead to higher productivity.

2. It has, according to Mr. Willis, significantly improved interactions with employees and peers for two of the three supervisors who studied and presented the model. (The third supervisor, who is nearing retirement, showed no appreciable change.)

The use of this model at Lincoln Electric, and in other contexts such as executive seminars, indicates that it has some value in explaining the complexity of productivity.

Model Limitations and Potential

The primary difficulty in practical usage of the model is that it is not currently possible to measure the behavioral and managerial factors quantitatively. Thus, the ability to predict or evaluate absolute levels of performance is beyond theoretical development. However, it *is* possible to evaluate the direction and relative impact of factor changes in an organization by combining (1) the model, (2) hypothesized behavioral relationships, and (3) partial quantification of organizational factors.

We believe that we have qualified worker productivity effectively; that is, we have shown relationships correctly at a proper level of complexity and aggregation. We suggest that the servosystem model of worker productivity provides a level of qualitative analysis needed to define, comprehend, and improve productivity. It forces managers and researchers alike out of the partial measure trap; it focuses concerns about measurement of productivity by demonstrating desired organizational goals and points of resource consumption; and it draws attention to the major factors that must be considered in developing productivity improvement programs.

First National Bank of Chicago

In a different type of application, the concept of the model structure was used to develop a representation of the determinants of quality in a bank. The project was part of a productivity audit of the lock box unit at First National Bank of Chicago (Hershauer 1978).

First National Bank of Chicago is among the largest banks in the country and offers a wide variety of services to its corporate customers, among them "lock boxes." Lock boxes free working capital, make funds available more quickly, and provide a receivables system service for corporate customers. In emphasizing the service aspect of lock boxes, the First National Bank of Chicago has allowed customers freedom in setting the details of each lock box account rather than forcing purchase of a standard form, and it has exercised the job enrichment program of the bank in individualizing responsibility for the complete handling of each account.

The key factors affecting quality in the lock box unit at First National Bank of Chicago are shown in Figure 6-8. Individual responsibility for accounts and a results-oriented managerial monitoring system appear to be the key design elements to maintaining the perceived high level of service quality. Pay, supervisory feedback, and group interactions do not appear to be closely associated with the effort to produce high quality in the lock box unit.

Except for the special application of the servo-system model to quality, the descriptive and normative models presented in these two chapters have not been directly concerned with improving service or product quality. The model that follows identifies the major factors that affect quality and depicts the inter-relationships among those factors.

RESEARCH CONCERNING OUTPUT QUALITY

The primary focus in productivity measurement and improvement has evolved around the quantity of inputs consumed, the quantity of outputs generated, and the associated costs. It is generally assumed (1) that productivity implies efficiency as measured in units consumed and produced and (2) that all outputs are of the desired quality levels (Bodoff 1975, vol. 2, p. 14). No specific attention is typically directed toward quality of inputs even though some attention is given to the quality of outputs. The effect of such reasoning on productivity measurement and improvement is such

Figure 6-8

Key Quality Factors in Lock Box

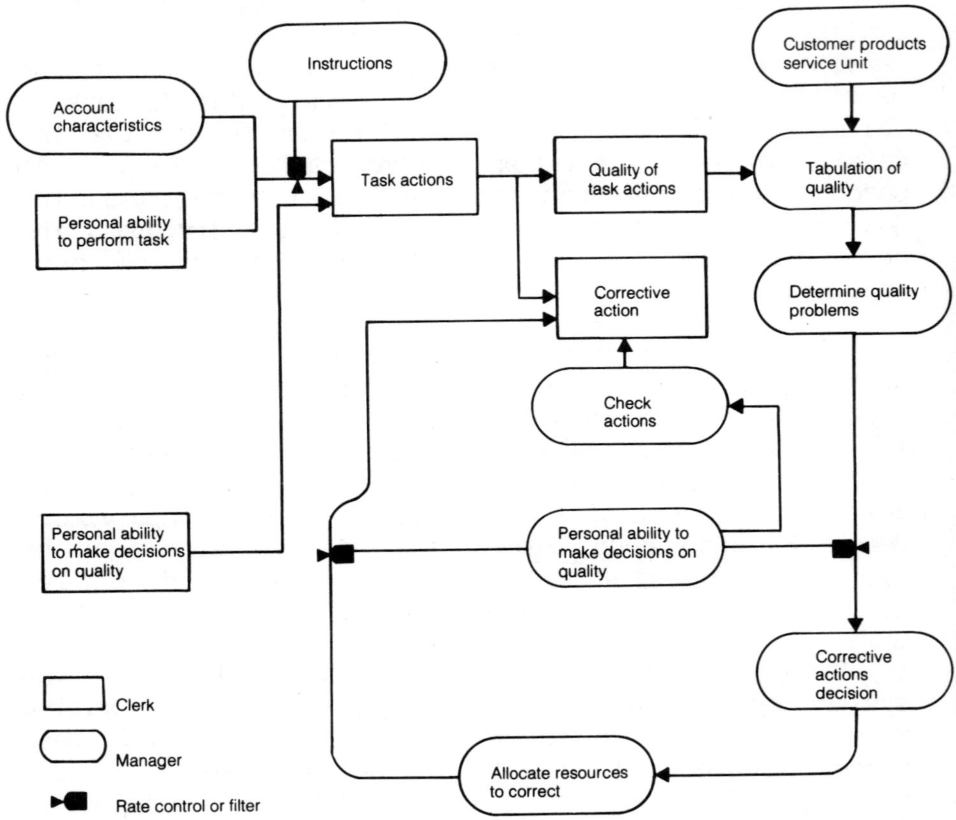

that the quality dimension of productivity remains unspecified.

Quality as a Dependent Variable

Scores of studies have been found that measure quality as a dependent variable. Generally quality is a secondary interest; quality data are only collected due to their availability. These studies usually set out to explain relationships between behavioral and economic independent varibles. Generalizations concerning quality, as quality relates to these independent variables, are difficult to make due to lack of consistent replication of the studies with quality data. This leaves those interested in factors relating to performance quality with partial research results at best.

Nevertheless, several technical and behavioral variables have been shown to have a systematic impact on performance quality. If the literature supports the view that these technical and behavioral variables affect performance quality, and do so to the extent that the same behavioral and technical factors affect productivity, then some insight into the quality dimension of productivity should result.

Technical Factors Affecting Quality

Accepting the technical factor-behavioral factor dichotomy of productivity modeling, the literature to be reviewed here concerns behavioral factors relating to the quality aspect of overall productivity. Before proceeding to behavioral factors relating to quality, a brief summary of the technical factors that affect quality is in order.

In production-operations management discussions concerning the quality of goods and services produced, it is generally agreed that errors are inherent due to process variation. Several technological factors contribute directly to errors and the subsequent quality level produced. Technical factors usually cited are (1) product design, (2) process design, (3) raw material and purchased parts, (4) equipment, and (5) tooling. Product design refers to the technical design of the product as it affects the way in which the product (or service) is produced. Process design includes overall facility design, work flow design, and job design. The raw material and purchased parts require quality specification and subsequent measurement upon receipt. Equipment and tooling are general indicators of the level of automation within the conversion process. The degree of scientific sophistication of each of these factors, as well as their interactions, certainly contributes to both the potential quality level and the achievement of that potential in the operation of the process.

Behavioral Factors Affecting Quality

The quality motivation and control literature revealed numerous behavior variables that seem to affect performance quality. Several of these behavioral factors are found to have quality data rather uniformly reported, at least uniformly enough so that some generalizations can be made. The behavioral factors from this review are (1) job characteristics, (2) job design, (3) instructions, (4) worker attitudes, and (5) contingency relationships.

Job Characteristics. Job characteristics and job design are quite closely related and could be considered as one factor under the general concept of task scope. Task scope (Schwab and Cummings 1976) is defined as incorporating both vertical (enrichment) and horizontal (enlargement) dimensions of the responsibilities and/or activities within a task. The two concepts have been separated here since studies relating to quality can be viewed from the perspective of *measuring* job characteristics that have a bearing upon quality as well as *prescribing* job designs that lead to improved quality.

Job characteristics have been identified and instruments for measuring these characteristics have been developed by Hackman and Lawler (1971) and Hackman and Oldham (1975). Hackman and Lawler, using four core task dimensions--variety, autonomy, feedback, and identity--found that the higher (more positively) that workers responded on the four core dimensions, the higher the *felt* pressure for high-quality work. Even more significantly, the employees also *produced* higher quality on jobs that rated high on all four core dimensions. These results did not hold for performance quantity; the four core dimensions did not relate to felt pressure for quantity or actual performance quantity. No negative relationship was evident; there was no relationship to quantity.

Schwab and Cummings (1976, p. 31), referring to the Hackman and Lawler study, presented the hypothesis that increases in task scope will increase the valence of performance. They further explained that this can be expected with respect to quality, but not to quantity.

Rigby (1970, p. 461) pointed out that error (and subsequent quality level) is a function of human variability:

> Error is a function of human variability; yet it is because man is so variable that he can learn, adapt, specialize, and serve all the roles, functions, and tasks that our society requires. Error and accomplishment are inseparable aspects of human nature. One does not err at that which he does not do. The illiterate do not commit reading errors. Yet that which man does is always susceptible to error.

Rigby suggested that people err because (1) they are capable of doing many different things in many different ways and (2) they are in a task environment where a large number of contributing factors can cause errors. The first factor, involving human capability, suggests a variability that doesn't exist when machines replace humans. Machine standardization (increased automation) is not necessarily the ultimate goal, however, as many tasks require human capability and variability to meet the preset quality standards. The second reason people err--the large number of possible contributing factors--as explained by Rigby, involves situation-specific analysis to determine the quality-related variables. In an unpublished study cited by Rigby involving people performing a printed wiring board assembly, Rigby had the workers systematically list all of the factors they thought could contribute to assembly errors. The result was an initial 328 factors that, after discussion, was reduced to 157 significant factors. These factors were behavioral and technical, all being <u>task specific</u> as perceived by the workers. The point made by Rigby is that human error is inherent when people are involved in productive work and that this effort is due to varying human capabilities and task-specific contributing factors.

The work of Hackman and Lawler and Rigby suggests that task characteristics do relate to performance quality. Rigby suggests that task-specific factors influence quality, and he provides evidence that workers agree. Hackman and Lawler are more specific; they found four specific task dimensions that affect performance quality.

Job Design. The task emphasis in quality performance leads us into the job design literature to determine if job enlargement and job enrichment affect performance quality. It is clear that, within bounds, job enlargement leads to increased productivity on a quantity dimension. This is especially true for jobs with short cycle times, times of a minute or less (Kilbridge and Webster 1966). The influence of enlargement and enrichment on quality deserves closer examination.

Biggane and Stewart (1972) in the Maytag study on job enlargement found improved performance quality in enlarged jobs accompanied by reduced inspection costs. Folloni (1971) in a case study on job enlargement studied one job; environmental conditions were controlled by varying only one task condition. He enlarged the job to include the task of "self-certification," a program whereby nearly all workers were able to certify their work as defect free. Over 2,000 employees were measured over a four-year period with results indicating (1) over a 40 percent reduction in defects, (2) over a 50 percent reduction in rework costs, and (3) a 58 percent reduction in defects per order. These studies tend to support job enlargement as a partial solution to improving performance quality. Job enlargement is especially helpful if jobs have been designed with low cycle times and if tasks added are quality oriented.

Job enrichment studies show a much clearer relationship to quality improvement than they do to quantity improvement. Adding a meaningfulness dimension typically increases the qualty level (Davis 1971; Englestad 1972; Felloni 1971; Janson 1975; Marks 1954; and Ruch 1968).

Engelstad, in explaining variance matrix techniques used in a paper mill in England, provided data that indicated a quality improvement due to (1) increased job responsibility, (2) increased interest by the employee in one's work, and (3) participation in technical changes in the job that enhanced quality. This increased quality was achieved without inreased material cost and with total labor cost being held constant in the study.

Davis (1972) added two job enrichment treatments in a large West Coast military industrial facility. The first was a product responsibility treatment. The second was a quality responsibility treatment that added inspection to the functions required to complete a product. The inspection included authority for final quality acceptance of products.

The technically complex product responsibility treatment resulted in a significant quality improvement, no cost reduction, and no productivity (quantity) change. The technically trivial quality responsibility treatment resulted in no quality improvement (but indications of improvement), a significant cost improvement, and no productivity (quantity) change. Overall, the enrichment treatments were successful on quality and cost dimensions without adversely affecting quantity. In another study Davis (1972) found mean quality of output to relate empirically to these job factors: (1) the employee's perception of job importance, (2) independence as to control of quality, (3) self-control of organization of work, including rate, and (4) peer communication. Generally, the more meaningful the job to the employee, the higher the quality level.

In a data processing environment in an insurance company, Janson (1975) found significnat quality improvement with job enrichment. Error rates dropped from 1.53 percent to 0.99 percent, and "outstanding" operators increased from 20 percent to 50 pecent while "poor" operators dropped from 11 percent to 5 percent of total operators. Marks (1954) added another dimension regarding job design and quality in a study that illustrated that individual job design when compared with line job design resulted in fewer errors (higher quality) with no significant difference in quantity or production costs. Ruch (1968), in the controlled behavioral laboratory, found that either an enlarged task or an enriched (more meaningful) task led to increased quantity and increased quality (decrease in percentage of errors). He also found that the job that was both enlarged and enriched resulted in higher quantity and quality levels than did either factor added alone.

The job design literature, specifically job enlargement and enrichment studies, leads one to conclude that (1) as jobs are enlarged and enriched, there is a more systematic affect on performance quality than quantity, (2) as jobs are enlarged and enriched, the quality level can be expected to improve, and (3) enriching jobs by adding individual quality-related tasks or responsibilities enhances performance quality.

Instructions. Instructions regarding tasks to be performed seems to have a definite impact on quality (Adam 1972; Vough 1975). Adam found that quality performance was better when initial instructions emphasized quality than when instructions made no mention of quality. In presenting a procedure used at IBM to improve productivity, Vough (ch. 6) emphasized the initial instructions as being critical in achieving high quality levels of performance. It seems logical that employees are especially attentive when introduced to a new job or task and quality emphasis in the initial instruction set would lead to increased quality performance.

Worker Attitudes. The relationship between attitudes and performance quality was not direct in most studies reviewed. In reviewing quality motivation literature, Adam (1973) found that criticism was directed toward zero defects-type attitudinal procedures of the American Society for Quality Control. Critics found no lasting changes in attitudes or quality improvement after about six months. In a diecasting firm study that was partially designed to examine whether attitudes or conditioning procedures would affect quality (Adam 1975), the question wasn't answered. In this study, when conditioning procedures were used in conjunction with an attitude change procedure, attitudes did not change and quality did not improve significantly, although there were some indications of improvement.

Davis, in a previously mentioned study, found that workers' perceptions of job importance affected performance quality. Hostage (1975), in reporting the quality control emphasis at Marriott Hotels, makes a good case for the employee's attitude affecting service quality delivered.

The conclusion is that studies are conflicting and there is no general support for a hypothesis expressing any clear attitude-performance relationship.

Contingency Relationships. Contingency relationships, within the framework of operant conditioning procedures, seem to hold some promise as a behavioral procedure for influencing the employee's performance quality (Adam and Scott 1971; Adam 1973; Adam 1975; Johnson 1975). In the controlled environment of the behavioral laboratory, the subject's quality response followed by appropriate reinforcement procedures appears to positively influence quality (Adam 1972; Johnson 1975). However, when applied in an ongoing organization environment, Adam (1975) achieved limited results on a quality dimension using conditioning procedures. Quality results varied depending upon the way in which quality was measured; overall quantity improved significantly and costs were reduced.

Productivity-Quality Modeling Research Studies

No literature was found that modeled productivity, quality, and measurement. The intent of the following section is to conceptualize the quality dimension of productivity. The model developed relates to the literature on productivity, quality, quantity, and measurement.

A BEHAVIOR-TECHNOLOGY MODEL OF FACTORS AFFECTING QUALITY

This model is based on the premise that several technical and behavioral variables have a systematic impact on performance quality. The methodology begins with performance quality and works backward through successive iterations to indicate chains of influential relationships among factors. These factors are then grouped according to their relationship to the organization and the quality of the organization's output.

Environmental Characteristics and Constraints

Before presenting the model in its entirety, it is necessary to place the model in its environmental context and to emphasize important interactions, constraints, and limitations (Figure 6-9). The basic elements of a business environment--legal and political, economic, technological, and social--have a strong, direct effect on the behavior-technology model of quality. The nature of that effect and its relative strength depends upon the particular firm or industry being modeled. For example, quality in the pharmaceutical industry may be more constrained by legal than by economic considerations, whereas for a small electronics manufacturer the opposite may occur.

These four environmental characteristics can be subdivided further to provide more clarification. In terms of the quality model to be presented here, the specific environmental elements and constraints listed in Table 6-1 are most relevant. These environmental characteristics and constraints must be considered an integral part of the model itself. Attempts to apply the model without due consideration to changing environmental interactions and limitations will fall far short of success.

Elements of the Model

The behavior-technology model of factors affecting quality begins with a basic dichotomy of quality goals: potential quality and actual achievement of that potential (Figure 6-10). Establishing potential quality is

Figure 6-9

Environmental Characteristics and Constraints

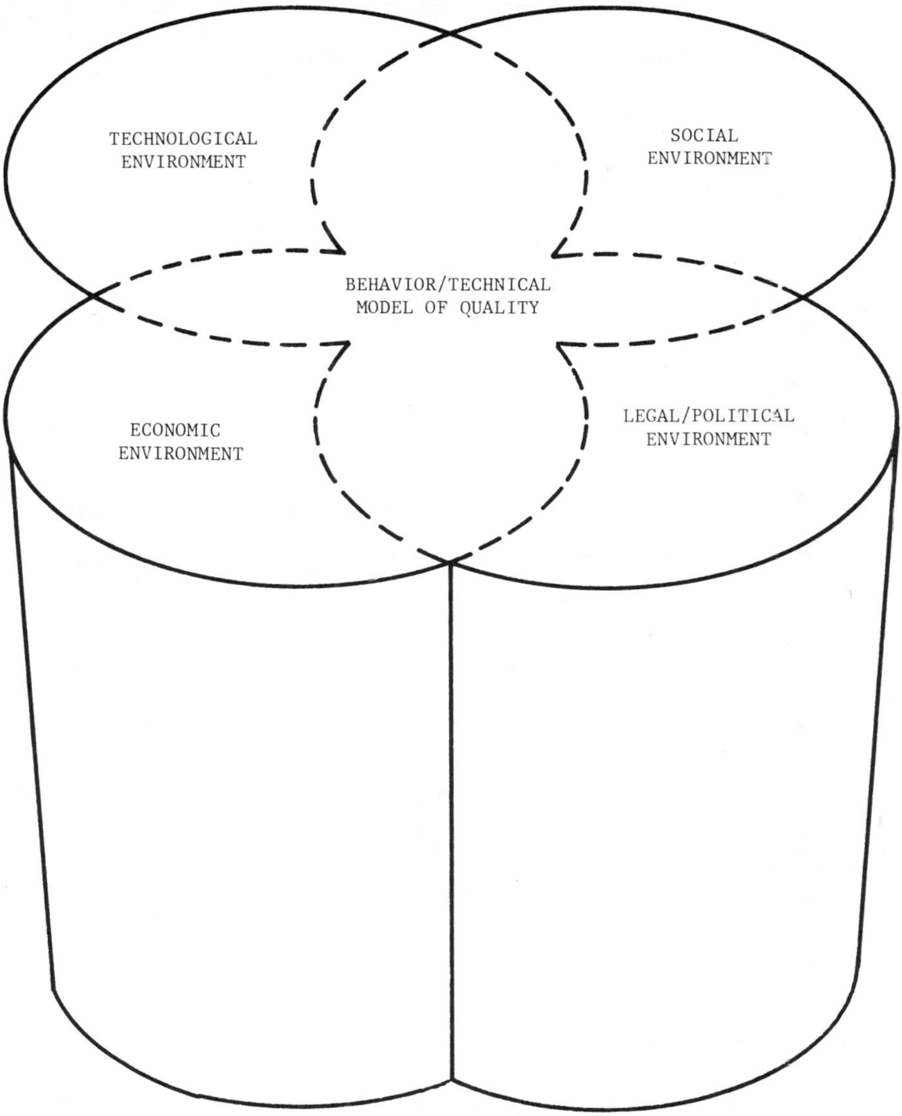

Table 6-1

Environmental Characteristics and Constraints

Environmental Characteristics and Constraints
Social environment
Personal value systems
Ethical considerations
Social responsibility
Taste and behavior patterns
Immediate community influence
Greater community influence
Legal-political environment
Regulatory agencies
National laws, local ordinances and restrictions
International considerations
Tax considerations
Consumer legislation
Union agreements
Technological environment
Basic and applied research results
Engineering knowledge
Management knowledge
Material-equipment innovation
Process innovation
Product innovation
Economic environment
General economic conditions
Labor market conditions
Vendor market conditions
Customer (competitive) market conditions
Inflation

Figure 6–10 The Dichotomy of Quality Goals

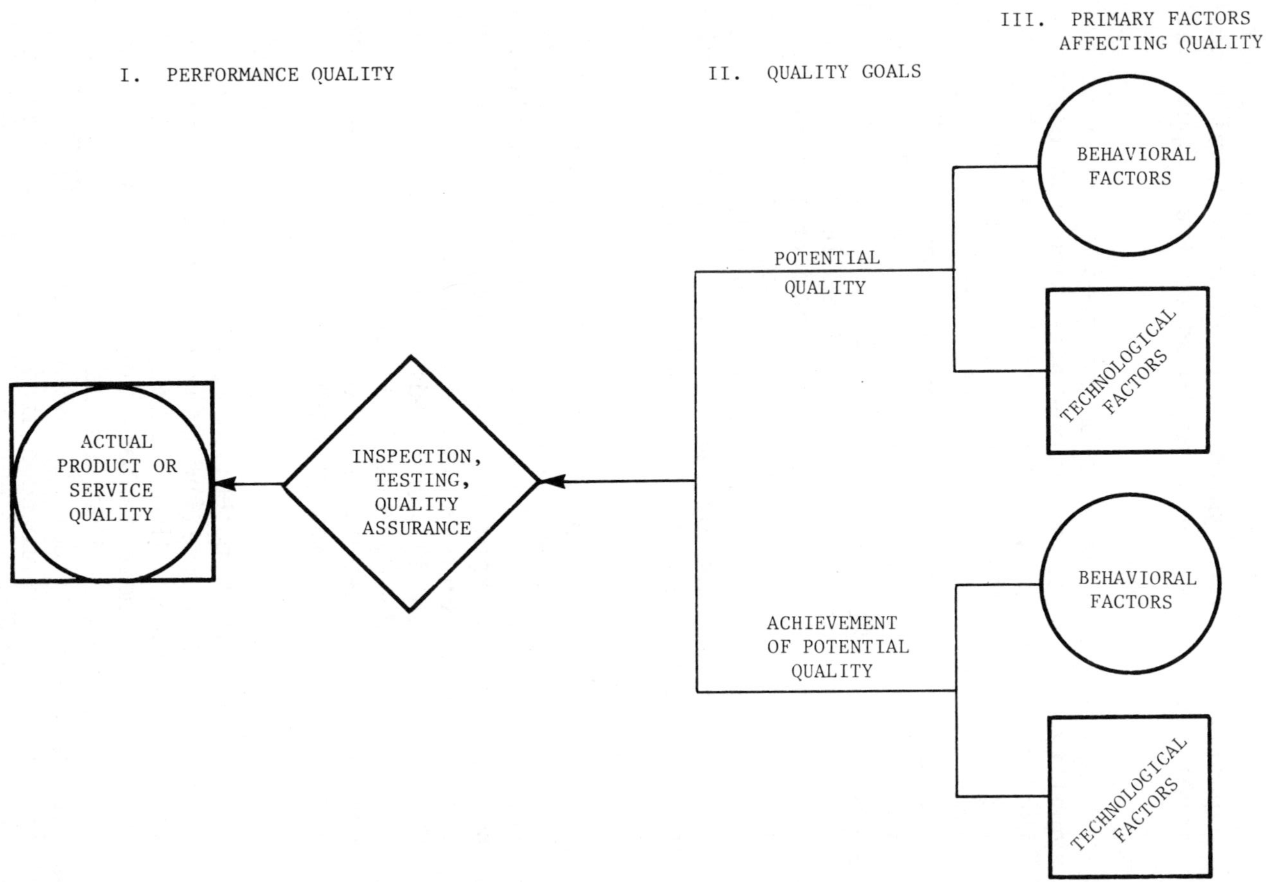

essentially a design or planning function. It involves the decisions about input factors that affect the capability of the system to produce at a given quality level. It places an upper bound on the output quality.

Actual quality can be no greater than potential quality, but poor decisions affecting the operation of the system can cause actual quality to fall short of its potential. Quality diagnosis must precede treatment. From a diagnostic point of view, a firm with poor overall quality may be suffering from one of two ills: (1) achievement of a low potential or (2) failure to achieve a high potential. Obviously, these ills demand different remedies. If the problem is a low potential, the system may need to be redesigned or perhaps a change in inputs is needed. The problem of failure to achieve a high potential results from a well-designed but improperly managed system. If so, operational policies and decisions should be reviewed and revised.

Between these goals and the actual quality is the inspection, testing, and quality assurance program of the organization. The program's primary function is to monitor the output and pass, reject, or screen the product or service to assure conformance to a standard. The responsibilities of diagnosing and correcting quality problems may reside in this unit, at some higher organizational level, or with operative workers, depending upon organization philosophy.

Derived from potential quality and achievement of that potential are the many controllable and uncontrollable factors that influence quality. It is useful to subdivide these factors into those that are technological and those that are behavioral. Primary factors affecting quality both behavioral and technological are, in most cases, influenced directly by some organizationally controllable variables. This, then, becomes the crux of the model (Figure 6-11), an illustration of the relationships that affect output quality. Management can now make planning and operating decisions that, through a chain of relationships, will affect output quality.

Factors Affecting Potential Quality

Potential quality is the quality level that the process, as designed, is capable of achieving under ideal operational conditions. It is a function of a great many design and input variables that have been combined and condensed into five primary factors, some technological and some behavioral. A few of these variables and their antecedents will be explained as typical of the others.

In discussions by production-operations managers concerning the quality of goods and services produced, it is generally agreed that errors are inherent due to process variation. Several technological factors contribute directly to errors and the subsequent quality level produced. Technological factors usually cited are: (1) raw material and purchased parts, (2) equipment, (3) tooling, and (4) the work environment (including process design, individual job design, and layout).

Although the evidence indicates that the work environment affects the potential output, it is insufficient to recommend that an organization "change its work environment." That directive is too general to lead to specific action. The factors that make up the work environment--design of the product, process, and jobs, selection of equipment and tooling, facilities location and layout, and purchasing practices--are recognized as decision variables over which the organization can exercise control.

Organizational controllables are not without constraints, however. Job designs are subject to limitations in the law (such as the Fair Labor Standards Act), limitations imposed by union agreements, and limitations imposed by the current state of technological development to name just a few examples. Similarly, other organizational controllables are constrained by other environmental characteristics, which may be social, economic, legal and/or political, or technological.

The right-hand margin of the model in Figure 6-11 outlines a simplistic representation of a very complex relationship. The arrows indicate that all

Figure 6-11

Behavior-Technology Model of Factors Affecting Quality

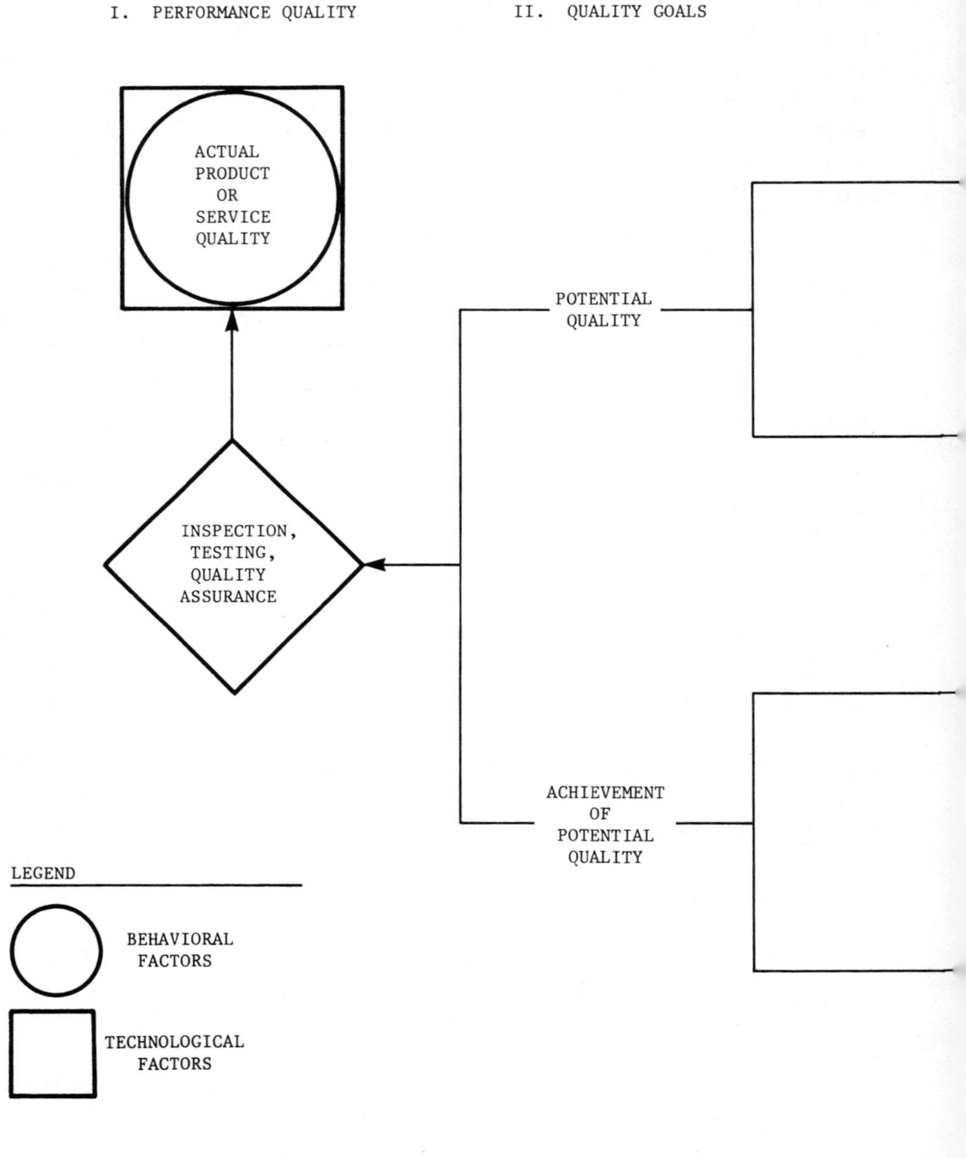

Figure 6-11 (continued)

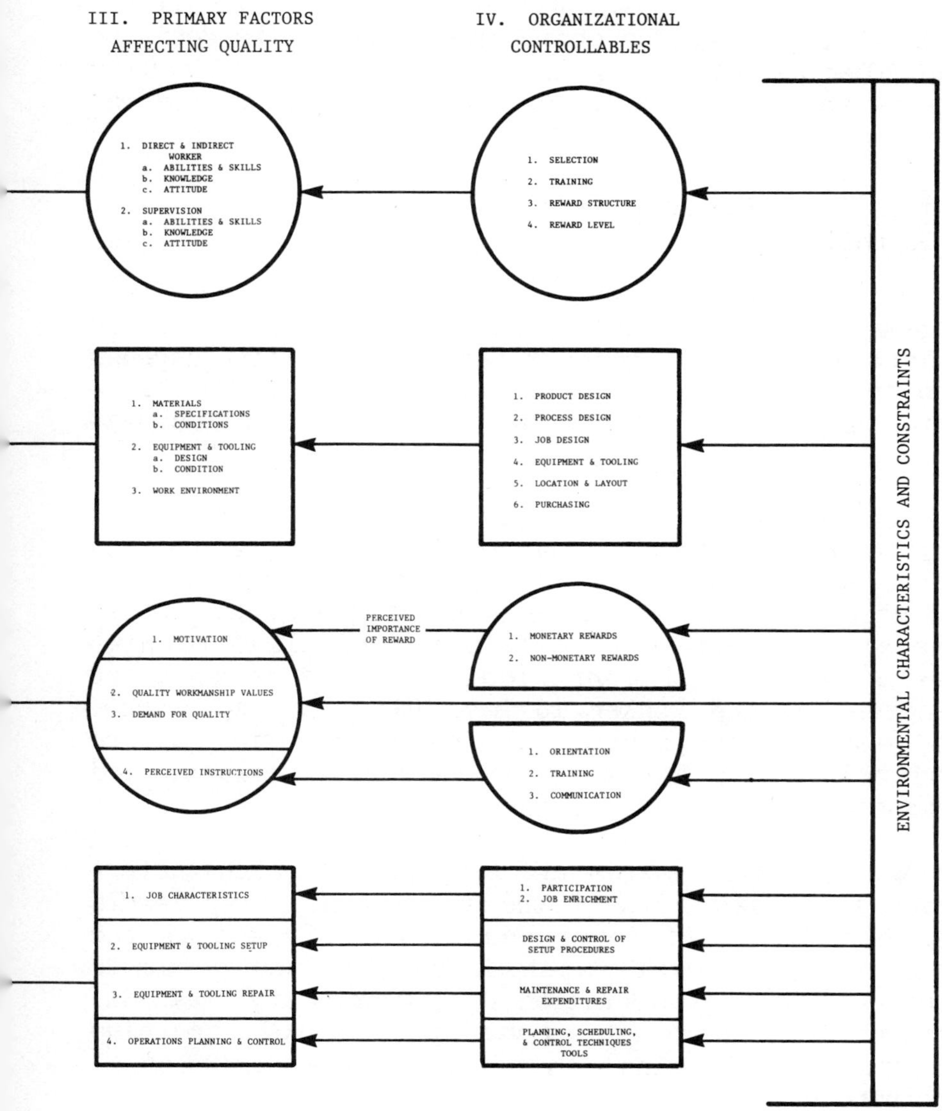

organizational controllables and some primary factors are influenced directly by forces in the environment, for example, OSHA regulations, changing social values, competitors' strategies, and technological innovations. In this framework, the organization varies its decision variables as one would adjust valves in a hydraulic network to assure the proper flow of output at the end of the process.

Factors Affecting Achievement of Potential Quality

Whereas the first quality goal--potential quality--is essentially a design of planning concept, the second quality goal--achievement of potential quality--depends upon techniques of management and controls. To illustrate this point, a behavioral factor, motivation, was chosen.

Scores of studies support the contention that achievement of potential quality is, in part, a function of the motivation of the worker. Motivation, in turn, has been the subject of decades of research. It is generally agreed that certain rewards lead to high levels of motivation provided that the rewards are perceived by the worker to have value or importance. The rewards under control of the organization can be subdivided into monetary or extrinsic rewards and nonmonetary or intrinsic rewards.

Again, these rewards are subject to the characteristics and constraints of the environment. Pay levels are bounded at the lower end by the law and at the upper end by social (status, equity) and economic (cost-benefit) considerations. Nonmonetary rewards, although more difficult to vary and control, are also motivation determinants subject to environmental constraints.

Summary of the Behavior-Technology Model of Factors Affecting Quality

The behavior-technology model of factors affecting quality begins with actual performance quality and traces the relationships of its antecedents: quality goals, primary factors, organizational controllables, and environmental characteristics and constraints. Two examples are detailed: one set of technological factors leading to potential quality and one behavioral factor relating to achievement of potential. Careful study of the remainder of the model will yield insights into other primary factors and the organizational controllables that affect them.

This model is speculative; it was not derived as a synopsis of the research literature but as a logical exercise drawing on both research and experience. The knowledgeable reader will recognize some paths through the network where ample empirical support exists and other paths where little supporting evidence is available.

In total, this model provides causal or antecedent relationships for a large number of factors previously treated independently. These factors are organized in a way that might foster greater understanding of the complexities involved and channel future research along productive paths.

SUMMARY

Two models were presented in this chapter that enumerated the factors involved in productivity. The models attempted to delineate the relationships among factors affecting productivity so that inferences could be drawn as to why productivity within the firm is high or low; and, more important, what variables can be changed to improve productivity.

The first model is a servosystem model of worker productivity (Figure 6-2) that is an extension of modeling in motivation and system dynamics. The focus of the second model changes from worker productivity to performance quality. After reviewing the research concerning output quality and the factors influencing quality, a behavior-technology model of factors affecting quality was developed (Figure 6-11). For both behavioral and technical factors, quality potential is identified and related to achievement of potential quality. The model suggests some interesting propositions and hypotheses that could be tested, the results of which should be quite useful to the practicing manager.

PART III
MEASUREMENT AS A BASIS FOR IMPROVEMENT

In the introduction to this book we noted the confusion surrounding the term "productivity" and subsequently developed a working definition. Much of this book has dealt with defining "quality" and developing a procedure for measuring quality as a productivity ratio. In the final chapter, we summarize the quality measurement procedure and discuss applications of the procedure. We would be remiss, however, if we did not again emphasize the need for productivity improvement. Although we've focused on productivity measurement, especially for quality, the ultimate goal is to improve productivity with a scorekeeping mechanism in place.

A measurement system serves two basic functions for productivity improvement programs. First, people perform to measures when rewards are linked directly to those measures. Research in psychology, operant conditioning, management by objectives, information systems, organization behavior, and incentive systems have verified this phenomenon repeatedly. Productivity measurement can itself be a productivity improvement program. Keeping score can lead to improvement in the score; we must keep score on the right factors to meet company goals. Second, the value of planned programs can be estimated only if specific measurement is possible. The effect of managerial changes can be determined subject to the net result on outputs <u>and</u> inputs as given in productivity ratios.

7 Quality and Productivity Conclusions

Economists, corporate executives, government leaders, academicians, and owners of small businesses have emphasized the current plight of productivity improvement in the United States as we enter the 1980s. The slowdown in U.S. productivity growth is one of the most significant economic problems in recent years--ranking with and related to inflation as a problem of national concern. A very good synopsis from the Federal Reserve Bank of Kansas City highlights the problem:

> Concern about the growth rate of productivity is well founded, for productivity growth is the major source of increase in our standard of living and one of the keys to the reduction of inflation. This statement becomes evident when the growth in real output is viewed as consisting of two parts, that due to the growth in inputs and that due to the growth in productivity, or output per unit of input.
>
> Looking at labor productivity and output in the private business sector, it may be seen that, from 1947 to 1967, U.S. business output rose at an annual rate of 3.7 per cent [Figure 7-1]. Over this same period, the number of people at work grew approximately 1.0 per cent per year. But because the number of hours per worker declined approximately

Figure 7-1

Output per Hour in Private Business Economy, 1947-1979
Actual Levels and 1947-1967 Trend (1967 = 100)

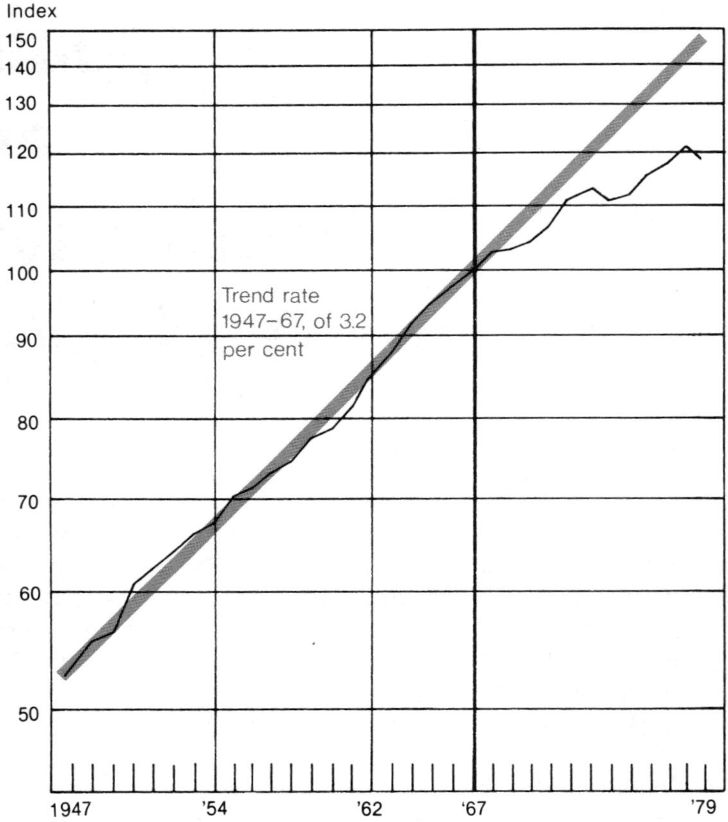

Source: Bureau of Labor Statistics.

*1979 value estimated.

0.5 per cent per year, total hours worked rose only 0.5 per cent annually. The difference between average annual output growth of 3.7 per cent and hours growth of 0.5 per cent is accounted for by the 3.2 per cent average annual increase in productivity. Thus, almost 90 per cent of the growth in real output in the U.S. from the end of World War II through 1967 was due to increased productivity.

Growth in productivity in recent years, however, has been much less vigorous. This is vividly illustrated by [Figure 7-1], which contrasts the growth path of actual productivity in the private business sector from 1947 to 1979:2 with the trend rate of productivity growth between 1947 and 1967. Even discounting the cyclical decline in productivity resulting from the 1973-1975 recession, there is no doubt that a distinct slowdown has taken place in the growth of productivity.

This slowdown is further illustrated in [Table 7-1], which presents labor productivity growth in several sectors of the economy for four time periods. Also provided are the growth rates of hours and output in the private business sector for the same periods. The marked slowdown in productivity growth in all sectors is obvious, as are its effects on the growth of output. In the private business sector, only the rapid growth in employment and hours worked kept the rate of output growth from slowing even more than it did. Over a 10-year period, the difference between productivity growth rates of 3.2 per cent (between 1947 and 1967) and 1.2 per cent (in the 1972-78 period) equals 22 per cent of the final year's output per hour. Thus, had output per hour grown at the 1947-67 rate each year through 1978, while hours grew at the rate they did, real GNP in 1978 would have been about $250 billion above its actual level of nearly $1,400 billion. (Zell 1979, pp. 13-26)

Factors relating to the productivity decline are discussed and explored in some depth by Zell. Among the more interesting variables seemingly related to productivity are "advances in knowledge" and "technological change" as manifested in investment in plant and equipment. Figure 7-2 illustrates the relationship between investment and productivity. Many of the

Table 7-1

Productivity Growth Rates for Major Sectors
(annual average percentage rates of change)

Sector	1947–1967	1967–1972	1972–1978	1977:4–1979:2
Private business	3.2%	2.2%	1.2%	–0.3%
Hours	0.5	1.1	1.8	3.5
Output	3.7	3.3	3.0	3.2
Nonfarm business	2.6	1.9	1.9	–0.5
Farm*	5.7	5.2	2.1	NA
Manufacturing	3.0	3.0	1.8	1.4
Durable	2.7	2.5	1.2	0.7
Nondurable	3.3	3.6	2.6	2.6
Nonfinancial corporations	3.2†	2.0	1.3	0.17§

Source: Bureau of Labor Statistics.

* From Joint Economic Committee Report 1979, No. 96–44, p. 56.

† 1958–1967. Earlier years not available.

§ 1977:4 to 1979:1.

NA = not available.

Figure 7-2

Investment and Productivity in the United States and Other Nations, 1960-1976

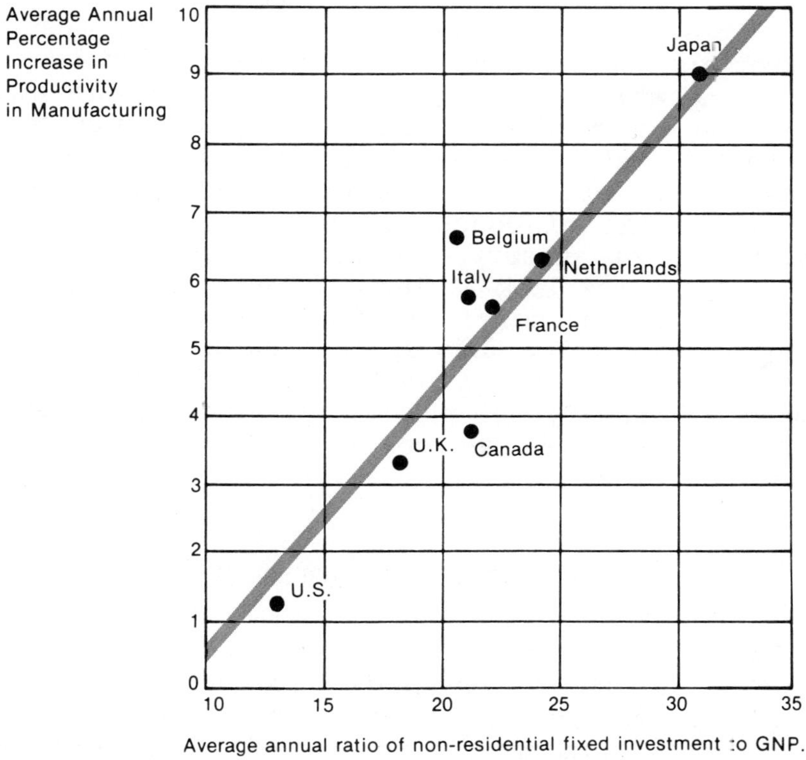

Source: Productivity Perspectives, American Productivity Center, Inc.

es cited in this book, including the development of ...lity-productivity measurement procedure, would be candidates for classification as "advances in knowledge" aimed at increasing productivity.

In most of the economic reviews of the issue of productivity decline, we find an absence of discussions concerning quality. Yet, from discussions with executives and observation of foreign product purchases in the United States (radios, television, household appliances, autos, etc.), we find quality as a major output characteristic of concern. Defining and measuring quality was the primary, but not sole, emphasis of this book. Let's now look at three features of quality and productivity in summary form: descriptive and predictive quality-productivity models, the measurement procedure for quality in a productivity framework, and a brief summary of quality and productivity measurement applications. Finally, the book is concluded with an eye toward the future.

DESCRIPTIVE AND PREDICTIVE MODELS

Rather than repeat the models presented in Chapters 5 and 6, let us briefly review two that we have been developing and that typify modeling efforts to date. These models help provide the conceptual understanding required for managers to design effective change programs that lead to improvement in productivity ratio values.

A Subjectively Scaled Productivity Matrix: A Descriptive Model

Ruch and Hershauer summarize their study of twelve recognized highly productive organizations and the matrix patterns of their scaled judgments as follows:

> For the selected "productive " organizations previously discussed, the dissimilar matrix patterns and the wide dispersion of characteristics on each of the scales indicate major differenes that may be explained by the notion that system interactions allow organizations to (1) use widely differing

programs to reach similar, individual and organizational responses or (2) use essentially the same program to reach vastly dissimilar individual and organizational responses. For example, all five rating levels were indicated by at least one organization on the "Selection Criteria for Management" scale. The twelve selected organizations ranged from selecting managers almost solely based on attitude to almost solely based on skills and also by all combinations in between these two extremes. The programs used to develop these managers would, therefore, have to differ according to the criteria by which they were selected. It is impossible to say that one selection criterion is "right" and the other is "wrong." But the specific implication for training and development, for example, is that their modus operandi must fit, in a systems sense, with the selection criteria and, indeed, with every other aspect of the organizational system.

Worker representation was spread fully across the scale from unified to diffused. This result indicates that the right mix of other factor levels will allow management to perform efficiently with or without unified and strong labor representation. Many managers and labor leaders alike will balk at such a suggestion since many managers feel that unions must be kept out at all costs, whereas some labor leaders feel that workers will be exploited without unified representation. Those organizations without unions that are models of high levels of organizational productivity and highly positive worker involvement and satisfaction contradict the latter opinion. And those organizations dealing with some of the strongest unions that are also models of high organizational and individual achievement contradict the first. Intervening variables must exist, and continuing studies of productivity should seek to further identify and explain these intervening variables in specific organizational contexts.

The differing significant statistical relationships found among individual factors, attitude factors, and individual performance measures for the seven organizations analyzed as productive systems provide empirical verification of the need for a contingency approach toward factors affecting productivity. Such differing results indicate that <u>interaction</u> effects of organizational and individual variables must be confounding these basic relationships. It must be kept in mind that the jobs examined in this study are so similar in nature that differences may be generally attributed to different management practices or individual attitude presets. It would be irresponsible, therefore, to develop "laws of productivity" that would apply to every situation. (Ruch and Hershauer 1974, pp. 115-116)

A Behavioral-Technical Quality Model: A Predictive Model

A behavioral-technical model of factors affecting quality was presented in Chapter 6 as Figures 6-10 and 6-11. In Figure 6-10 we observe that performance quality is a function of both the potential for quality and the achievement of that potential. Establishing potential is primarily a design and planning activity; achievement of that potential is a labor-management activity. Both potential and achievement have behavioral and technological factors that impart quality.

Figure 6-11 illustrates how quality goals are influenced by factors directly affecting quality (column III). Some of these factors are controllable by the organization (column IV). The entire model elements--organizational controllables, primary factors affecting quality, quality goals, and performance quality--are all influenced and modified by environmental characteristics and constraints. This model attempts to set out variables that the organization can control through design, planning, and effective management. Although a great deal of literature exists to support separate components of the model, many hypotheses could be established and tested to verify and perhaps modify the model. In particular, further investigation of the behavioral-technological interactions and resulting impact on performance quality hold substantial promise for productivity gains. For the manager seeking productivity improvement, the model identifies key elements and relationships that must be included in quality productivity changes.

A MEASUREMENT PROCEDURE FOR QUALITY IN A PRODUCTIVITY FRAMEWORK

The result of a recent study on quality measurement was a prototypical approach for creating a measurement system for the quality dimension of productivity. Table 7-2 summarizes the steps in this procedure presented in detail in Chapter 3. The procedure was tested in the Federal Reserve Banking System for check processing and personnel functions as presented in Chapter 4.

Table 7-2

Quality Measurement Procedure Activities

Activity Sequence	Activity
1	Decide to measure productivity (top management)
2	Select project coordinators
3	Familiarize project coordinators with system (function)
4	Select participants; divide into groups
5	Define system and establish boundaries
6	Determine unit operations
7	Generate deviations; select and rank deviations
8	Finalize key quality deviations
9	Generate key quality deviation measures
10	Collect technology and systems input data
11	Transform measures into productivity ratios and indicators
12	Present transformed measures to participants for clarification
13	Put measures into questionnaire format
14	Rank measures
15	Produce final quality-productivity ratios

Face Validity of the Measurement Model

Participation. Perhaps the most positive evaluation of the measurement model is that systems participants understood the process and could respond to all of the requests. Systems boundaries were readily established, and unit operations were established that were virtually the same when set by differing employee pairs.

As we follow the procedure of Table 7-2, the next step required participants to generate deviations for the unit operations through a structured group process called the nominal group technique (NGT). Deviations represent variations from norms or standards. The literature on the nominal group technique indicates that a successful session should produce over 25 factors. Participants in all groups were certainly able to respond successfully to the required task.

In check processing, first- and second-site groups produced 50 and 87 deviations, respectively. In personnel, first- and second-site groups produced 39 and 53 deviations, respectively. In selecting key quality deviations, participants were asked to select and rank the top 5 deviations. The NGT group process normally results in a concentration of votes on 3 to 6 items. For the selections of key quality deviations in check processing, 6 deviations and 3 deviations were stressed at the first and second sites, respectively. In personnel, the numbers were 5 and 6, respectively. Finalization of key quality deviations was accomplished by the project coordinators and then presented to participants. The number of key quality deviations ranged from 7 to 13 and coverage was provided for all unit operations.

The last major group task was to generate possible measures for the deviations. Again, the process worked well. First and second sites in check processing produced 69 and 60 measures, respectively. First and second sites in personnel produced 47 and 68 measures, respectively. Additional measure information was obtained by questioning participants about technical subsystems used.

The group sessions using participative methods on site were found to be quite successful in obtaining needed information to produce a set of productivity measures for the quality of service.

Measure Selection. The final stage of the measurement approach involves an independent effort by the project coordinators. The information on deviations and measures is put into sets of possible productivity ratios and productivity indicators for each key quality deviation. For check processing, the result was a set of 75 measures for the first site, with a maximum of 9 measures and a minimum of 4 measures for a single deviation. The corresponding numbers for the second check site were 35, 8, and 2. For personnel, the result was a set of 70 measures for the first site, with a maximum of 10 measures and a minimum of 4 measures for a single deviation. The corresponding numbers for the second personnel site were 74, 11, and 1.

All of the measures at a particular site were put into a questionnaire. Organizational participants were asked to evaluate each of the measures by completing the questionnaire. Scoring of these evaluations allowed acceptance of measures receiving an average response from participants of a median evaluation or better. This final scoring of productivity measures provided an overall evaluation of the process. For the first and second sites in check processing, 41 and 25 measures were accepted, respectively. For personnel, 48 and 36 measures were accepted at the first and second sites, respectively. Each deviation was covered by at least one accepted measure; most had more than one accepted measure. The average number of accepted measures per key quality deviation was 3.6, with a maximum of 7 for any single deviation.

The participants' acceptance of measures as reflected in the responses to the measure evaluation questionnaire was a strong plus for the reasonableness of the approach. Fifty-nine percent of the suggested measures were accepted. Additionally, consistency in cross tabulations for an acceptance rate reflected the strength of the approach in different settings. Sixty percent of check-processing measures were accepted; 58 percent of personnel measures were accepted; 61 percent of first-site measures were accepted; 56 percent of second-site measures were accepted.

Evaluations of the Measurement Process

Probably the most significant evaluation of field tests is that the process works. Participants are able to understand the process, families of measures are produced for key quality deviations, and a high percentage (60 percent) of measures are accepted. The process works in a service function such as personnel, and it works for a quasi-manufacturing function such as check processing. The procedures also worked well in second sites for each of the two functions.

The ability of the process to yield systems-wide measures in addition to measures for each deviation was demonstrated at the first check processing site. Six system measures were listed for final evaluation; five of these were accepted by system participants. These total department quality measures are listed in Table 7-3. Of the five accepted measures, two are output-to-input ratios and two are proportions of resources consumed for deviations. The fifth is a proportion of volume processed that is affected by the deviations. The two productivity ratios are stated as percentage of error-free items divided by cost or labor hours. The nature of these five systems-wide measures is characteristic of the accepted measures throughout. A few other accepted measures are unidimensional levels of some important environmental or systemic variable.

The process can thus be expected to yield a mixture of (1) output-to-input productivity measures, (2) proportions of total input usage devoted to deviations, (3) proportions of volume affected, and (4) levels of some important related variables. In addition to being multidimensional, productivity measurement also appears to be a loose collection of multiple constructs. The evidence supports use of a family of measures for the quality dimension of productivity. Although it may be unwise to force multiple dimensions into a single index, it is certainly theoretically and pragmatically feasible to do so. However, it is infeasible to combine a set of multiple construct measures into a single index.

Table 7-3

Total Department Quality Measures for Check Processing, Bank A

Numerator	Denominator	Average Score
D-1 Percentage of error-free outgoing cash letters	Total labor hours in check processing	.276†
D-2 Dollar amount of "as of" adjustments	Total dollars processed	.062†
D-3 Percentage of cash letters not causing correspondence and phone calls	Cost per 1,000	-.150
D-4 Percentage of error-free outgoing cash letters	Cost per 1,000	.104†
D-5 Total dollar expense of adjusting key deviations	Total dollar expense in check processing	.294†
D-6 Total labor hours in adjusting key deviations	Total labor hours in check processing	.222†

†Accepted; score greater than +.050.

Requirements for Quality Measurement Model Usage

Top management support within and immediately above the systems boundaries is a necessity. Some confusion with the process at the second personnel site must have been at least partly caused by very minimal involvement of the manager immediately above the systems boundary top level. In addition, the top manager within the system did allow a few interruptions in group procedures that were not experienced at other sites. However, expressed confusion over some parts of the process did not seem to deter achievement of an excellent family of measures for apparently reasonable key quality deviations.

Time is the primary investment required by an organization to create a family of measures for key quality deviations. The effort would normally require at least an eight-week elapsed time commitment.

The cost for participant involvement is a minimum allocation of 40 person-days to the project. The times required of the various participants in the process are:

1. ten days for each coordinator
2. two days for each member of group B (daily operations managers)
3. one day for each member of group A (top systems managers)
4. two additional days for the top manager within the system
5. one day of facilitator and/or analyst time to assist with key quality deviations and/or final productivity measurement package

The availability of the data required to implement the accepted measures has not been determined. The frequency and cost of operating a reporting system for accepted measures is unknown at this time. However, it is obvious from the nature of many of the measures that data would be available and that costs would not be extensive for several of the accepted measures. Implementation of the total set of accepted measures would have to be coordinated with managerial styles and organizational policy setting for each specific site. Our experiences in subsequent applications (reported in the next section) suggest that the ten days for each coordinator is high. One coordinator has been satisfactory, with the organization providing clerical support.

Concluding Thoughts on the Quality Measurement Procedure

The major result of the project was the development of a measurement process for the quality dimension of service departments. The implementation and usage characteristics of the measurement model will be demonstrated in the follow-up usage of the technique in situations like those just described.

In conclusion, a number of key points regarding the nature of the prototypical measurement process must be remembered. First, the focus is on quality rather than quantity. Second, the process is concerned with measurement and the identification of key areas needing managerial action. Third, the process is based upon the assumption that the knowledge necessary to create measures exists in the minds of current system members. Thus the process provides the structure and emphasis necessary to develop productivity measures for the quality dimension. Structured group processes and sociotechnical systems analysis provide the conceptual framework for obtaining participation and emphasis in measurement. Fourth, the robustness of the process has been demonstrated by application in two dissimilar service functions within a quasi-governmental service organization. The process worked in the two functions and generated extensive and complete results.

The resulting measurement scheme provides multidimensional coverage of multiple constructs. Unit operations, deviations, key quality deviations, and a family of measures for the key quality deviations are all obtained. The unit operation and deviation data provide a wealth of information useful for enhancement analysis. The accepted family of measures includes productivity ratios, proportions of resource usage, proportions of volume affected, and indicator variable levels.

SUMMARIES OF QUALITY AND PRODUCTIVITY APPLICATIONS

The applications of quality and productivity measurement that we have selected to summarize are grouped by <u>function</u>, <u>product or service</u>, or <u>the entire firm</u>.

Functional Applications in Services

Federal Reserve Banking System Check Processing. Results for quality measurement in check processing were presented in the previous section of this chapter and in Chapter 4.

Federal Reserve Banking System Personnel Departments. As with check processing, results from application of quality measurement were presented in this chapter and in Chapter 4.

The Transfer of Funds (Wire Transfer) Function in Commercial Banking. The Bank Administration Institute has underway an application of the quality measurement procedure in the transfer of funds function in commercial banking.[1] A steering committee of bank officers suggested transfer of funds as a critical area for quality within banks since an incorrect transfer can be very costly to a bank. The initial phase was conducted at each of three commercial banks of varying size. Each bank went through the quality measurement procedure described in Chapter 3.

The largest of the three banks experienced about 5,000 money transfers (by wire) per day that average $2 million each. Clearly, when $10 billion a day flows through a bank, quality is of paramount importance, as transfer errors can result in lost interest for one or more days and perhaps on rare occasions a loss in the funds. The largest of the three banks employed 100 full-time equivalent employees in this function.

The second phase of the project was to bring the managers of all three banks together and compare the unit operations, deviations, and measures generated and accepted by each bank. In a joint work session, a common set of measures was selected. The third phase involved an industry questionnaire to allow most of the hundreds of banks with wire transfer functions to

---

[1]The Bank Administration Institute, Park Ridge, Illinois. Support from Ronald G. Burke, president, and operations staff David Smith, Walter Stafeil, and David Taylor resulted in this application.

collect data on a few quality measures. That phase is currently underway.

One of the measures resulting from the study is presented as equation 7-1. The deviation (source of variation) in the process is an "incorrect or incomplete recording of information requesting a transfer of funds." The initiation of a transfer frequently is a telephone conversation, and errors in recording data can and do occur. The quality productivity ratio (QPR) is

$$\text{QPR} = \frac{\text{Number of wire transactions with correct information initially recorded}}{\left[\text{Total number of wire transactions}\right]\left[\text{cost to record a wire transaction}\right] + \text{interest paid due to recording errors} + \text{dollar income lost from recording errors} + \text{dollar labor cost to correct recording errors}} \quad (7\text{-}1)$$

This study illustrates that measures can be established across organizations--provided that the function is generally the same in different organizations. These measures are expected to be the first phase in developing a data base for quality standards among banks of similar size and scope in the transfer of funds function.

<u>The Automation Systems Department at the Honeywell Large Information Systems Division (LISD).</u>[2] The objective of the project at the Honeywell LISD was to identify productivity measures, not just quality measures, for a large and diverse department called Automation Systems. This department's purpose was to support and improve the efficiency of manufacturing through automation hardware and software development

---

[2]Special thanks go to John Blair and Stan Williams of Honeywell LISD for participation in and release of this project.

and maintenance. The project was exploratory and did not include specific plans for implementation of measures or improvement procedures. The prototypical procedure was applied with only minor addition of a clarification session prior to administration of the measures questionnaire. A facilitator was used. The facilitator's company position was to act as a liaison between automation systems and manufacturing.

Definition of system boundaries required considerable effort to identify the multiple facets of both demand and outputs. Demand comes primarily from manufacturing, quality engineering, and internally proposed projects and includes:

1. need to support new and enhanced products
2. need to support new and enhanced factory processes
3. need for new and enhanced information systems
4. any requests for service (hardware, system studies, maintenance, and support software)
5. system malfunctions
6. obsolete equipment and software

Output was defined as several parts, such as (1) software, (2) hardware, (3) service, (4) training, (5) documentation, (6) proposals, (7) advanced techniques, and (8) technical papers. Taken together, these parts yield a general output: a system that does something for somebody when needed. Organizationally, the boundaries included four of five functional areas assigned to Automation Systems, twelve groups under the area managers, and the analysts, programmers, engineers, and technicians. Major interactions are with manufacturing, quality engineering, and computer operations.

Although the department dealt with both hardware and software and participants were dubious about a common set of unit operations, a very reasonable set of unit operations generally relating to any systems development and support staff function was developed. They are given in Table 7-4. Key deviations for these nine unit operations are shown in Table 7-5. Remember that these deviations refer to both quantity and quality dimensions. Table 7-6 includes, for each deviation, an example measure that was accepted following the final questionnaire evaluation.

Table 7-4

Unit Operations

Demand: Recognized need or problem		
	Unit Operation	Exiting Throughput State
U-1	Assign A.S. coordinator and analyze	Conceptual system solutions
U-2	Define concepts and estimate costs	Approved system proposal
U-3	Plan, formulate, and schedule	Project plan for system (conceptual specifications)
U-4	Analysis	Detailed system, functional specifications
U-5	Design	Detailed design
U-6	Develop and create system	Untested complete system
U-7	Test and debug	Functioning system
U-8	Qualify, document, train, and deliver	Qualified and installed system
U-9	Monitor operation and adjust	System that does something for somebody when needed

Table 7-5

Automation Systems Key Deviations

Description	Location(s) Introduced
1. Creativity of individuals	All
2. Change in project priorities	U-4, 5-8
3. Interproject synchronization and meshing	D, U-1, 2-8
4. Morale	All
5. Work distribution	U-5, 6-8
6. Demand on time by other projects	U-1, 2-9
7. Practicality of schedules	D, U-3
8. Lack of trained personnel (capability training)	U-2, 3-7
9. Changes in personnel	All
10. Computer availability and response	U-6, 7
11. Influence of interacting groups	D, U-1, 4-8
12. Changes in project scope	All
13. Nonproductive effort (such as some paperwork and meetings)	All

Table 7-6

Example Measures for Key Deviations

Deviation Number	Measure	
	Numerator	Denominator
1	Effective lines of code delivered	Total programming hours used
2	Percentage of projects started with an approved project plan	Labor hours spent on planning
3	Hours spent on "work around" solutions	Total project hours used
4	Satisfaction index from attitude survey	Costs to conduct survey plus costs to conduct training and seminars plus personnel costs to receive training and complete survey
5	Percentage of time lost due to support system failure	None
6	Percentage of hours spent on scheduled tasks	Labor hours spent on planning
7	Variation of actual hours from estimated hours	Labor hours spent on planning
8	Modules completed per unit of time	Modules planned to complete per unit of time
9	Cycle-up hours (start-up time) spent on activities	Total project hours used
10	Average transaction response time	None
11	Percentage of projects completed by original schedule date	Hours spent in transactions with interacting groups
12	Percentage of projects completed without scope change	Project hours allocated to U-1, 2, 3
13	Total personnel hours charged to projects	Total hours paid

The reactions of the division director over Automation Systems, the manager of Automation Systems, and the ten additional staff members who participated in the project were positive. They were extremely cooperative with the process, appreciative of the communications channels opened by the process, and approving of the resulting measures. Only the practicality of gathering needed data for a few of the measures was questioned.

A project to implement computer reports of selected and practical measures from the approved set has been instigated. Two university student interns were hired by Honeywell to learn the internal computer system and then to assist the external project coordinators in installing the measurement system. Although the student interns were employed, the measurement system has not yet been implemented in a complete system. However, several of the indicators have been installed and are currently reported and monitored. For example, the measures listed for deviations 5 and 8 in Table 7-6 are in use. Additionally, John Blair of Honeywell LISD stated that the procedure ". . . provided an excellent insight into the operations and allowed [indicated areas for] improvement through process and procedure change."

McDonnell Douglas Astronautics Company. The quality measurement procedure presented in this book was applied with the production planning group at McDonnell Douglas Astronautics Company with two important modifications.[3] The primary work of this planning group is to transform engineering specifications and drawings for missiles and space hardware into manufacturing instructions for product and/or purchased parts. In the first modification the group was asked to generate both traditional productivity measures (efficiency ratios; quantity measures) and quality measures. This lengthened the procedure and measure set somewhat, but resulted in a more complete set of measures for the service function.

---

[3]McDonnell Douglas Astronautics Company-St. Louis, St. Louis, Missouri. The authors would like to acknowledge Robert E. Perkins, Director of Manufacturing Engineering, Walt Ezyk, Manager of Industrial Engineering, and McDonnell Douglas for providing this example from their applications.

The second modification was that two users were incorporated into group B, the group that was involved in the procedure throughout. This procedural change also worked quite well, giving users a better understanding of the production planning function and providing those in production planning with an appreciation of user problems. Users included in the process were a foreman from manufacturing and a shop production control staff person.

Table 7-7 illustrates the linkages throughout the process identification and final measurement procedure. One step in the production planning process, the unit operation planning instructions, provides the example. Note that the first measure is a traditional productivity ratio of labor output over labor input while the second measure is a quality productivity measure reflecting good pieces as output over the sum of processing and correction costs as inputs. The second measure is not dimensionally the same in both denominator and numerator, as is the first measure.

Product or Service Applications in Services

Consumer Checking Accounts at North Carolina National Bank.[4] The Bank Administration Institute in cooperation with North Carolina National Bank has applied the prototypical quality measurement of Chapter 3 to the service of processing consumer checks and servicing the accounts. The service begins when a customer asks to open a checking account, includes processing the checks accounting for funds in the checking account, and ends by notifying the customer through a bank statement of account activities. Unit operations identifying these and other operations were generated by a cross section of branch, operations, and marketing personnel following the specified procedure. Deviations were identified, measures were selected, and

---

[4]The authors would like to acknowledge Bedford Boise, Senior Vice President of Operations, Donald F. Allen, Assistant Vice President, and North Carolina National Bank for their cooperation and willingness to share information.

Table 7-7

Application of Quality and Quantity Measurement for a Production Planning Function in Aerospace Manufacturing

Step in Measurement Procedure	Group Generated Output
Identify demand	Demand: Requests for manufacturing bill of materials, tooling, and work procedures (requests from engineering for analysis and from manufacturing for direct support)
Unit operation	U-1: Planning work instructions
Key deviation	D-1: Incorrect and/or incomplete engineering
Quantity productivity ratio (PR)	$\dfrac{\text{Number of pieces of planning initiated as revisions to drawings} \times \text{standard hours per revision} \times \text{standard labor rate}}{\text{Actual labor hours for total pieces of planning initiated as revisions to drawings} \times \text{actual labor rate}}$
Quality productivity ratio measure (QPR)	$\dfrac{\text{Number of pieces of planning completed correctly}}{\left[\text{Total number of pieces of planning completed} \times \text{labor and computer cost to process a piece}\right] + \left[\text{number of pieces of planning corrected or revised due to engineering} \times \text{cost per item to correct or revise planning}\right]}$

several measures were implemented. Data are currently being collected on the measures. Table 7-8 provides a synopsis of one unit operation, deviation, and measure from this application. The procedure worked well, and there seemed to be a side benefit of communication facilitation between functions since the focus was on service rather than on any one function within the organization.

Don F. Allen, Assistant Vice President, made the following comments on how quality-productivity ratios were useful in one instance:

> In monitoring the preparation of new checking account source documents I noticed a sudden drop in the QPR ratio for the main office. However, the QPR ratio for the preparation of new checking account source documents at our branch office continued to increase. This immediately indicated to me that it was not a keypunch problem since both locations' source documents are keypunched in the same area. I checked with the manager of our Main Office Customer Service personel and found that there had been a change in personnel and that due to inexperience a number of errors were being made in preparing the source document. We were able to identify the errors and share the information with the new employee so corrective action could be taken. This certainly enabled us to identify and respond quickly rather than going under the assumption it was keypunch errors and hopefully would improve over a period of time.

Quality Measurement for the Firm

Commercial Banking. First National Bank of Atlanta and Northwestern National Bank of Minneapolis were presented in Chapter 2 as case examples of quality measurement and quality-productivity ratios.[5] Northwestern

---

[5]The authors would like to acknowledge Thomas G. Goodrum, First National Bank of Atlanta, and Victor A. Schwinghamer, Northwestern National Bank of Minneapolis, for their willingness to share quality procedures and results.

Table 7-8

Application of Quality Measurement for a Personal Checking Account in a Commercial Bank

Step in Measurement Procedure	Group-Generated Output
Identify demand	Demand: Customer requires convenient safe-keeping and transfer of funds
Unit operation	U-1: New account documents prepared
Key quality deviation	D-1: Source document not completed correctly or in timely manner
Measure (QPR)	$\frac{\text{Number of source documents completed correctly}}{\text{Total number of documents completed} \times \text{cost to open personal checking account} + \text{number rejected source documents} \times \text{cost to reject source documents}}$
Actual measure (Jan., 1980)	$QPR = \frac{162}{(168)(\$0.90) + 30(\$0.75)}$ $= \frac{162}{\$172.80 + \$22.50}$ $= 0.83$ units output per dollar of resource

National Bank has added the unique feature of pyramiding measures. If management is willing to set a quality standard, then all measures can be converted to a percentage of standard and added or compared directly within and between departments. Conceptually, one total quality measure can emerge for the firm. Many alternatives exist other than equal weighting and adding of the percentages for quality attributes. At Northwestern National Bank a quality control manual explains measurement and information that is available.

Yet another feature of Northwestern's work in quality is the organization of a staff department, the Productivity and Quality Analysis Section. Productivity analysis (work measurements, establishing standards, other traditional industrial engineering techniques) has been successfully combined with quality control (quality measurement, quality standards, and other traditional sampling and control methods). Both are active in <u>assisting</u> line managers by providing expertise, information, and techniques that influence productivity (efficiency) and quality.

First National Bank of Mobile, Alabama, has developed a quality-productivity measure for each of several functions in the bank, including zip code sorting, encoding errors (proofing), check filing, and wire transfer.[6] The measures follow one of the modified quality-productivity ratio forms presented in Chapter 2. Administrators at the bank report that they have found the measures very useful in tracking performance quality and taking management action based on measured quality results.

Productivity Measurement at General Telephone and Electronics (GTE)

GTE Data Services developed a productivity measurement system for measuring data processing (Peeples 1978). The data processing activity at GTE involves

---

[6]The authors acknowledge Rod M. Favis, First National Bank of Mobile, Alabama, for his willingness to provide information.

managing 14 data centers for as many individual telephone companies. The measurement system was implemented in data centers ranging in size from an IBM 360/40 shop with 22 people to a site with three IBM 370/165s and 300 people. The system involves measures for efficiency as well as effectiveness (quality). Of particular interest was a system acceptable to customers as well as management--forcing a focus on errors and timeliness.

Experience indicated that within operations computer operations would be easier to measure than the systems development process, so implementation of measurement began there.

The productivity measurement and improvement program is basically one of awarding "points" for meeting goals. Effectiveness in supporting outside departments was weighted more heavily than computer efficiency--a significant point for many data processing centers where it is "easier" to reverse these criteria in importance.

Rather than focus on details of the measures, which are in the referenced article, let's look at the overall results. Even though no specific improvement program other than measurement was used, in five years the productivity measurement scheme assisted in a 39 percent improvement in productivity. Managers apparently managed to the measures. This example of measuring companywide productivity across 14 data centers necessitated a small initial investment in software and required five person-days per month and some machine time to maintain. The costs seem reasonable when compared with the return.

Quality Control at Marriott

Hostage reviews the points in Marriott's quality control program that rank the lodging-food services firm among the most respected in the industry (Hostage 1975). A key feature appears to be the development of performance standards for management and the service employees. Written, highly detailed statements of expected productivity are prepared for each member of management. Similarly, booklets are prepared to guide the performance of lower-level employees with standards of performance stressed. A team of inspectors travels about the system evaluating units to see if productivity standards are being met. The overall thrust of Hostage's message is behavioral. He concludes by stating that "it takes happy employees to make happy customers"--a simple conviction that is quite possibly true for a broad range of services with high employee-customer contact.

CONCLUSIONS

The issue of declining productivity increases in the United States is an unresolved problem at the current time. Our judgment is that quality is a slighted component in most productivity improvement efforts. You must have the ability to measure quality by relating outputs (good items or services) to the resources required to obtain those outputs. In this book we have presented one approach to developing these measures (Chapter 3).

We do know that the quality measurement procedure works. Chapters 2, 4, and 7 have provided examples of quality-productivity ratios that were developed with this procedure and are being applied. Quality measurement is but a start toward quality improvement--yet a necessary step if improvement is to be systematically assessed. This quality measurement procedure is simple and participative and, with a reasonable expenditure of time and money, generates actual quality-productivity measures. The real payoff, however, remains with improvement. If managers work to improve the measure values, they can focus on key areas for needed change as identified by the measurement process.

The modeling efforts of Chapters 5 and 6 hold additional promise for improvement. It is our opinion, however, that if managers, behavioral scientists, operations research specialists, industrial engineers, and others interested in productivity improvement within the organization will start measuring quality systematically as they make changes, then we will learn a lot more about improving quality and the relationship between quality and key behavioral and technological variables. This empirical approach should add substantially to our ability to model and seek improvement.

Our position toward quality and productivity has not changed substantially since our research efforts began in the 1970s. We still believe that productivity improvement is critical, that managers can do something about improvement, and that quality is a definite part of the total productivity improvement effort. Our side-stepping into quality measurement has been a needed part of the more critical and interesting issue of productivity and quality improvement.

References

Adam, E. E., Jr. "An Analysis of the Change in Performance Quality Employing Operant Conditioning Procedures," Journal of Applied Psychology, 56 (December 1972), 480-486.

______. "New Dimensions in Quality Motivation," American Society for Quality Control Technical Conference Transactions (May 1973), 314-318.

______. "Behavior Modification in Quality Control," The Academy of Management Journal, 18 (December 1975), 662-679.

______. "Quality and Productivity in Delivering and Administering Public Services," Public Productivity Review, 3, no. 4 (Spring/Summer 1979), 26-40.

Adam, E. E., Jr., and R. J. Ebert. Production and Operations Management: Concepts, Models, and Behavior. Englewood Cliffs, N.J.: Prentice-Hall, 1978.

Adam, E. E., Jr., J. C. Hershauer, and W. A. Ruch. Measuring the Quality Dimension of Service Productivity. National Science Foundation, Grant No. APR 76-07140. Washington, D.C.: U.S. Department of Commerce, NTIS, PB282243/AS, 1978.

Adam, E. E., Jr., and W. E. Scott. "The Application of Behavioral Conditioning Procedures to the Problems of Quality Control," The Academy of Management Journal, 14 (June 1971), 175-193.

Biggane, James F., and Paul A. Stewart. "Job Enlargement: A Case Study," in Design of Jobs, pp. 264-276, eds. L. E. Davis and J. C. Taylor. Baltimore, Md.: Penguin, 1972.

Bodoff, Joan. The Effect of Innovation on Productivity in the Service Industries (Vol. 1: Summary Report; Vol. 2: Analytical Paper; Vol. 3: Annotated Bibliography). National Science Foundation, Grant No. RDA 75-20597 A01. Washington, D.C.: U.S. Department of Commerce, NTIS, PB 247-722, August 1975.

Chapple, E. D., and L. R. Sayles. The Measure of Management. New York: Macmillan, 1961.

Chase, R. B. "A Review of Models for Mapping the Socio-Technical System," AIIE Transactions, 7 (March 1975), 48-55.

Cleland, David I., and William R. King. Systems Analysis and Project Management (2nd ed.), pp. 271-277. New York: McGraw-Hill, 1975.

Cocks, Douglas L. "The Measurement of Total Factor Productivity for a Large U.S. Manufacturing Corporation," Business Economics, 9 (September 1974), 7-20.

Craig, Charles E., and R. Clark Harris. "Total Productivity Measurement at the Firm Level," Sloan Management Review, 14 (Spring 1973), 13-29.

Davis, L. E. "The Design of Jobs," in Design of Jobs, pp. 299-327, eds. L. E. Davis and J. C. Taylor. Baltimore, Md.: Penguin, 1972.

Davis, L. E., and P. H. Engelstad. "Unit Operations in Socio-Technical Systems: Analysis and Design," unpublished paper. London: Tavistock Institute of Human Relations, Document No. T-894, 1966.

Davis, L. E., and J. C. Taylor, eds. Design of Jobs. Baltimore, Md.: Penguin, 1972.

Delbecq, André, Andrew Van deVen, and David Gustafson. Group Techniques for Program Planning. Glenview, Ill.: Scott, Foresman, 1975.

Dodge, H. F., and H. G. Romig. Sampling Inspection Tables--Single and Double Sampling. New York: Wiley, 1944.

Dunlap, John R., and Vasilii P. Diatchenko. Labor Productivity. New York: McGraw-Hill, 1964.

Engelstad, P. "Socio-Technical Approach to Problems of Process Control," in Design of Jobs, pp. 299-327, eds. L. E. Davis and J. C. Taylor. Baltimore, Md.: Penguin, 1972.

Fein, Mitchell. Rational Approaches to Raising Productivity. Norcross, Ga.: American Institute of Industrial Engineers, 1974.

Follini, J. R. "Production Certifies the Quality of Its Work," Industrial Engineering, 3 (November 1971), 10-17.

Forrester, Jay W. Industrial Dynamics. Cambridge, Mass.: M.I.T. Press, 1961.

Foster, M. Developing an Analytical Model for Socio-Technical Analysis. London: Tavistock Institute for Human Relation, TIHR Doc. No. 7, 1967.

Fuchs, Victor R., ed. Production and Productivity in the Service Industries. New York: Columbia University Press, 1969.

Greenberg, Leon. A Practical Guide to Productivity Measurement. Rockville, Md.: BNA Book, 1973.

Hackman, J. R., and E. E. Lawler III. "Employee Reactions to Job Characteristics, Journal of Applied Psychology Monograph, 55 (June 1971), 259-286.

Hackman, J. R., and G. R. Oldham. "Development of the Job Diagnostic Survey," Journal of Applied Psychology, 60 (April 1975), 159-170.

Hanes, Lewis F., and Charles H. Kriebel. Research on Productivity Measurement Systems for Administrative Services: Computing and Information Services, APR 75-20546. Washington, D.C.: National Science Foundation, July 1978.

Heaton, Herbert. Productivity in Service Organizations. New York: McGraw-Hill, 1977.

Herbst, P. G. Task Structure and Work Relations. London: Tavistock Institute for Human Relation, TIHR Doc. No. 528, 1959.

______. Socio-Technical Design: Strategies in Multi-Disciplinary Research. London: Tavistock Publication, 1974.

Herbst, P. G., and I. Getz. "Work Organization at a Banking Branch Towards a Participative Research Technique," Human Relations, forthcoming.

Hershauer, J. C. "A Productivity Audit of Lock Box Service Quality," Bank Administration, 54 (October 1978), 43-48.

Hershauer, J. C., and W. A. Ruch. "A Worker Productivity Model and Its Use at Lincoln Electric," Interfaces, 8 (May 1978), 80-89.

Hershauer, J. C., W. A. Ruch, and E. E. Adam, Jr. "Quality Measurement for Personnel Services," American Society for Quality Control Technical Conference Transactions, Atlanta, Georgia, May 1980, pp. 262-269.

Hill, P. Toward a New Philosophy of Management. London: Gower, 1971.

Hinrichs, John R. Practical Management for Productivity. New York: Van Nostrand Reinhold, 1978.

Holzer, Marc, ed. Productivity in Public Organizations. New York: Kennikat Press, 1976.

Hostage, G. M. "Quality Control in a Service Business," Harvard Business Review, 53 (September-October 1975), 98-118.

Institute for Social Research, University of Michigan. Michigan Organizational Assessment Package: Progress Report II. Ann Arbor, August 1975.

Janson, Robert. "A Job Enrichment Trial in Data Processing in an Insurance Organization," in The Quality of Working Life, Vol. 2: Cases and Commentaries, pp. 300-314, eds. Louis E. Davis and Albert B. Cherns. New York: Free Press, 1975.

Johnson, George A. "The Relative Efficacy of Stimulus versus Reinforcement Control for Obtaining Stable Performance Change," Organizational Behavior and Human Performance, 14 (December 1975), 321-341.

Juran, J. M. "Quality Problems, Remedies and Nostrums," Industrial Quality Control, 22 (June 1966), 647-653.

Katzell, R. A., and D. Yankelovich. "Improving Productivity and Job Satisfaction," Organizational Dynamics, 3 (Summer 1975), 16-26.

Kendrick, John W. Understanding Productivity. Baltimore, Md.: Johns Hopkins Univesity Press, 1977.

Kendrick, John W., and Daniel Creamer. Measuring Company Productivity, rev. ed. New York: The Conference Board Studies in Business Economics, No. 89, 1975.

Kendrick, John W., and E. S. Grossman. Productivity in the United States: Trends and Cycles. Baltimore, Md.: Johns Hopkins University Press, 1980.

Kilbridge, M. D., and L. Webster. "An Economic Model for the Division of Labor," Management Science, 12 (February 1966), B255-B269.

Kilmann, R. H., and I. I. Mitroff. "Qualitative versus Quantitative Analysis for Management Science: Different Forms for Different Psychological Types." Interfaces, 6 (February 1976), 17-27.

Lawler, E. E., III. Pay and Organizational Effectiveness: A Psychological View. New York: McGraw-Hill, 1971.

Likert, Rensis. New Patterns of Management. New York: McGraw-Hill, 1961.

Marks, A. R. N. "An Investigation of Modification of Job Design in an Industrial Setting and Their Effects on Some Measures of Economic Productivity," doctoral dissertation, University of California, Los Angeles, 1954.

Meissner, M. Technology and the Worker; Technical Demands and Social Processes in Industry. San Francisco, Calif.: Chandler Publishing, 1969.

Mitchell, V. F. "Expectancy Theories of Managerial Motivation," Proceedings of the Academy of Management (August 1971), 210-220.

Monczka, Robert M., Phillip L. Carter, John H. Hoagland, and Lawrence W. Foster. Purchasing Performance: Measurement and Control, APR 75-20557. Washington, D.C.: National Science Foundation, August 1978.

Morris, William T. Productivity Measurement Systems for Administrative Computing and Information Services (Vol. 1), APR 75-20561. Washington, D.C.: National Science Foundation, 1977.

National Center for Productivity and Quality of Working Life. Improving Productivity: A Description of Selected Company Programs, Series 1. Washington, D.C., December 1975.

______. The Future of Productivity. Washington, D.C., Winter 1977.

National Commission of Productivity. Productivity. Report of the Commission. Washington, D.C.: GPO, 1972.

National Science Foundation RANN Program. Proceedings of the Grantees' Conference on Research on Productivity Measurement Systems for Administrative Services, ed. William A. Ruch. Washington: NSF Grant # APR 76-83866, November 1976.

Peeples, Donald E. "Measures for Productivity," Datamation, 24 (May 1978), 222-228.

Porter, L. W., and E. E. Lawler. Managerial Attitudes and Performances. Homewood, Ill.: Irwin, 1968.

Rigby, Lynn V. "The Nature of Human Error," in Transactions of Annual Technical Conference American Society for Quality Control, Pittsburgh, Pa., May 1970, pp. 457-466.

Roberts, Nancy. "Teaching Dynamic Feedback Systems Thinking: An Elementary View." Paper presented at the National ORSA/TIMS Meeting, Las Vegas, Nevada, November 1975.

Ross, John P., and Jess Burkhead. Productivity in the Local Government Sector. Lexington, Mass.: Lexington Book, 1974.

Ruch, William A. "The Effects of Changes in Stimulus Complexity on Routine Repetitive Task Performance," doctoral dissertation, Indiana University, Bloomington, 1968.

______, ed. Proceedings of the Grantees' Conference on Research Productivity Measurement Systems for Administrative Services. Tempe, Az.: National Science Foundation, November 1976.

Ruch, William A., E. E. Adam, Jr., and J. C. Hershauer. "Developing Quality Measures for Bank Operations," Bank Administration, 55 (July 1979), 47-52.

Ruch, William A., and James C. Hershauer. Factors Affecting Worker Productivity. Tempe: Arizona State University, 1974.

Schwab, Donald P., and L. L. Cummings. "A Theoretical Analysis of the Impact of Task Scope on Employee Performance," Academy of Management Review, 1 (April 1976), 23-35.

Shaw, John C. The Quality-Productivity Connection in Service Sector Management. New York: Van Nostrand Reinhold, 1978.

Shaw, John C., and Ram Capoor. "Quality and Productivity: Mutually Exclusive or Interdependent in Service Organizations?" Management Review, 68 (March 1979), 25-28, 37-39.

Shewhart, W. A. Economic Control of Quality of Manufactured Product. Princeton, N.J.: Van Nostrand, 1931.

Siegel, Irving H. Company Productivity. Kalamazoo, Mich.: W. E. Upjohn Institute for Employment Research, 1980.

Siegel, Sidney. Nonparametric Statistics for the Behavioral Science. New York: McGraw-Hill, 1956.

Smith, Ian G. The Measurement of Productivity (2nd ed.). New York: McGraw-Hill, 1969.

Stewart, William T. "A Yardstick for Measuring Productivity," Industrial Engineering, 10 (February 1978), 34-37.

Sutermeiser, Robert A. People and Productivity (1st ed.). New York: McGraw-Hill, 1963.

______. People and Productivity (3rd ed.). New York: McGraw-Hill, 1976.

Taylor, Bernard W., III, and K. Roscoe Davis. "Corporate Productivity--Getting It All Together," Industrial Engineering, 9 (March 1977), 32-36.

Taylor, Frederick W. Principles of Scientific Management. New York: Harper, 1911.

______. "The Principles of Scientific Management," paper presented at the First Conference on Scientific Management, The Amos Tuck School, Dartmouth College, Hanover, N.H.: October 1911.

Taylor, J. C. "The Human Side of Work: The Socio-Technical Approach to Work System Design," Personnel Review, 4 (Summer 1975), 17-22.

Taylor, J. C., and D. G. Bowers. The Survey of Organizations. Ann Arbor: University of Michigan, CRUSK/Institute of Social Research, 1972.

Taylor, J. C., et al. The Quality of Working Life: An Annotated Bibliography. Los Angeles: University of California at Los Angeles, 1973.

U.S. Department of Labor, Bureau of Labor Statistics. The Meaning and Measurement of Productivity. Washington, D.C.: GPO, September 1971.

______. Productivity: A Selected Annotated Bibliography (Bulletin 1776). Washington, D.C.: GPO, 1973.

Vaniel, Barry J., and Dan Wilson. "Defining and Measuring Productivity: An Operational Approach," paper presented at the AIIE Systems Engineering Conferences, Las Vegas, Nevada, November 1975.

Vough, Clair F. Tapping the Human Resource. New York: AMACOM, 1975.

Vroom, V. H. Work and Motivation. New York: Wiley, 1964.

Wyckoff, D. Darryl. "Issues of Productivity," Reprinted from Traffic World issues of September 18, November 6, 13, December 18, 25, 1972, and February 26, 1973. Distributed by Regular Common Carrier Conference, Washington, D.C.

Zell, Stephen P. "Productivity in the U.S. Economy: Trends and Implications," Economic Review, Federal Reserve Bank of Kansas City, November 1979, pp. 13-26.

Index